GUIDE TO
LETTER WRITING

K. Graham Thomson, FRGS, was a freelance journalist, an author and a lecturer in English. For sixteen years he was an assistant editor on the *Nottingham Guardian*, before moving to Fleet Street, where he served for twenty-one years on the editorial staff of the Press Association. As 'Dr Syntax' he contributed a weekly column on good writing to *World's Press News* for fifteen years, and to *John O'London's* for five years. He wrote part of *The Practice of Journalism* and a large part of the history of the Air Training Corps; he was also among the first radio broadcasters. Mr Thomson died in 1972.

Guide to
LETTER WRITING

K. Graham Thomson FRGS

revised edition
Pan Books London and Sydney

First published 1961 as *The Pan Book of Letter Writing*
by Pan Books Ltd, Cavaye Place, London SW10 9PG
6th printing (revised) 1970
9th printing 1976
© K. Graham Thomson 1961, 1970
ISBN 0 330 13023 4
Printed in Great Britain by
Richard Clay (The Chaucer Press) Ltd, Bungay, Suffolk

CONTENTS

CONTENTS

FOREWORD

The Purpose of this Book

LETTER WRITING for pleasure—the pleasure of writing and the pleasure of reading—was one of the chief occupations of the educated few in the 17th, 18th and 19th centuries, reaching its peak as a fine art in the 18th. Today, in the 20th century, it is said to be a lost art. The interchange of long letters full of family news and comments on public affairs has been replaced by the long telephone conversation or the short visit by car.

Nevertheless, there are still people who enjoy exchanging news by correspondence, and there is an ever-growing mass of business and official letter writing, all of which has been speeded and increased by the development of airmails. The world's postal departments handle thousands of millions of letters every year.

This book deals with personal, official and business correspondence, and covers the field as widely as possible. Care has been taken to use simple language and short words, and to explain technical terms where their use is unavoidable.

Section 1 offers general guidance on writing letters, and after analysing a letter, goes on to give detailed information about each of its parts.

Section 2, which deals with the writing of applications for employment, may be for some readers the most important section of the book. It has been written with the help of some of the largest employers of labour in Great Britain, and the advice obtained should be worth studying and following.

Section 3 deals with addressing people whose rank or position calls for some special style. The use of the correct style is a courtesy which should not be disregarded; and many a private citizen organising some good work for charity has had to face the problem of how to direct a letter to a mayor or a bishop correctly.

Section 4 deals with letters for particular occasions—offering condolences or congratulations, conveying invitations or expressing thanks. It also contains information on several points which are often overlooked.

The other Sections deal with common errors, punctuation,

7

plurals of foreign words that have been adopted into English, and a very condensed revision course in the parts of English Grammar which are of particular use in the composition of letters.

Included is a comprehensive reference section, which covers the special signatures of Anglican bishops, equivalent ranks in HM Forces and notes on abbreviations.

Tackling the problem of how to apply for a job from the other end, so to speak—by enlisting the aid of several employers—was an entirely new idea. Another new idea produced section 9, which lists the native names of countries with English translations. This is the first and only book published in England to contain such a list. Although a good number of model letters will be found in the book to illustrate the guidance given, it has been thought unnecessary to give many samples. A letter is essentially a personal production, and mere copying deprives it of its reality as an expression of the writer's personality. Moreover, the purposes for which letters are written are of such infinite variety that it is impossible to provide model letters to suit every circumstance.

It must be stated that all the letters given as examples, and all the names used throughout the book, are entirely imaginary.

Similarly, with regard to English composition, it has been thought unnecessary to overload the book with grammar lessons, exercises or tests, or textbook dissertations on the analysis of sentences and the parsing of words. The general aim of the author has been to provide help for those who are not accustomed to writing letters: information and guidance for those who wish to write letters well: and a useful office or home reference book for those who have to write letters often.

FOREWORD TO REVISED EDITION

CERTAIN CHANGES which have occurred since first publication of this book (*eg*, changes in the composition of the House of Lords) have been embodied in this edition.

The book has also been enlarged by the inclusion of notes on privilege and precedence and the addition of a list of administrative county towns, and an index to the whole book.

References to educational attainments in model letters applying for jobs have been brought up to date; and many additions have been made to other sections.

THANKS

THE AUTHOR gratefully acknowledges his debt and offers his thanks to the following companies, whose officers have very generously helped him with advice and information which is incorporated in Section 2 of this book:

> Albert E. Reed & Co., Ltd
> The Dunlop Rubber Co., Ltd
> The Ford Motor Co., Ltd
> The General Electric Co., Ltd
> Shell Petroleum Co., Ltd

and one of the 'Big Five' British banks, whose officer requested that its name be not mentioned, although useful advice was willingly given.

It must be stated that the names of their correspondents were not disclosed to the author by any of these companies. And, although Section 2 is based on, and embodies, advice given by representatives of these companies, the author is solely responsible for the form in which it appears in his book.

The author thanks the editorial staff of Pan Books Ltd, and particularly Mr C. A. E. Paget, and Miss Toni Blatt, for much valuable advice and help. He also thanks Mr E. F. G. Prior, who helped in the revision of Section 2; and Mr P. Cutlack for a suggestion used in Section 4.

Finally, the author gratefully thanks officers of the General Post Office, London, for much useful help, and also thanks the librarian of the Royal Geographical Society, London, the librarian of the United States Information Service, London, and officials at Canada House, London, for their assistance.

HOW TO WRITE LETTERS

A GOVERNMENT department concerned with separation allowances in wartime is alleged to have received the following letter:

> Dear sir,
>
> I am sending my marriage certificate and six children. I had seven and one died which was baptised on half a sheet of paper by the Rev. T——.

Another letter alleged to have been received by the same office read:

> Dear sir,
>
> I am writing these lines for Mrs J—— who cannot write herself, she expects to be confirmed next week and can do with it.

Whether true or not, these examples show how difficult it can be for people who are unused to writing to express clearly on paper the thoughts and problems in their minds. Letter writing, like any other art or craft or activity, requires two basic things: knowledge and practice. The aim of this book is to impart some, at least, of the necessary knowledge: it is for the reader to put it into practice.

A letter must convey the writer's thoughts, ideas, wishes, orders, opinions—according to its particular purpose—clearly, concisely, correctly and, perhaps, interestingly, movingly, sincerely. Lack of education, or the lapse of time since the writer left school, may make the writing of a letter difficult: the memory may no longer retain either the words required or the rules for using them correctly.

Moreover, many people lack the ability to think clearly, or to express their thoughts exactly: and this accounts for many of the misunderstandings that arise between people, some of the actions for libel that entertain the courts, and a good deal of the humour of books and periodicals.

The fundamental aims of good writing are the same for the author of a book as for the journalist writing in a newspaper, or for you and me when we write a letter. They are—to use words so clearly and precisely that the writer's ideas are easily and correctly understood by the reader; and to choose the words and arrange them in such a way that the result will give the reader pleasure, or arouse his interest, or persuade him to do what the writer wants.

To do this, the writer of anything—book, article, letter—needs knowledge: knowledge of words, their meaning and spelling—called vocabulary; knowledge of the uses and relationships of words—grammar; knowledge of the correct arrangement of words—syntax. In addition, a writer needs to discipline himself to compel his mind to formulate his thoughts in words and phrases which precisely express his meaning.

Almost everybody writes letters, although some do so so rarely that they are practically incapable of expressing themselves on paper at all—as the two examples given on the first page show.

Some letter writers have been precocious children who have later become famous men or women. Thomas Babington Macaulay (1800–59) who became an essayist, historian, politician, poet and a peer, was a twelve-year-old schoolboy when he wrote a letter home beginning:

My Dear Mama,
    I must confess that I have been a little disappointed at not receiving a letter from home today. I hope, however, for one tomorrow. My spirits are far more depressed by leaving home than they were last half year. Every thing brings home to my recollection. Every thing I read, or see, or hear, brings it to my mind. You told me I should be happy when I once came here, but not an hour passes in which I do not shed tears at thinking of home. . . .

He may have been a tearful, homesick small boy, but he wrote clearly, concisely and correctly; and how well he conveys his meaning to the reader!

Some poets were precocious little poets, such as Thomas Love Peacock (1785–1866), who wrote satires, novels and lyrics while working as a clerk and examiner in the service of the old East India Company. He was only nine when he wrote a letter home in verse, which began:

Dear Mother, I attempt to write you a letter
In verse, tho' in prose I could do it much better;

> The Muse, this cold weather, sleeps up at Parnassus,
> And leaves us poor poets as stupid as asses. . . .

and concluded, in typical schoolboy fashion:

> The bard craves one shilling of his own dear mother,
> And, if you think proper, add to it another.

No one could more clearly and concisely, not to say winningly, ask for extra pocket money, and one hopes that his quaint plea met with a satisfactory response. He made, however, an error in the last two lines, in changing from the third person *his* to the second person *you*. The last line should have been written

> And if she thinks proper, may add yet another.

However, he was only nine, so he had not yet had time to delve very deeply into the mysteries of grammar and syntax.

Macaulay, at twelve, wrote short, clear sentences which plainly conveyed his meaning. 'I hope, however, for one tomorrow.' 'Every thing brings home to my recollection.'

Another master of English prose who knew the value of crisp writing was Sir Winston Churchill. The careful choice of words, the brevity and tension of the sentences, make his volumes of history, memoirs and essays easy and gripping to read.

To write clearly, whether in a book or a letter, one needs to know words—their meaning, their spelling and how to arrange them in the best sequence. For those who wish to revise or to extend their knowledge of English grammar and syntax, Section 6 of this book contains a summary; and separate sections deal with punctuation, the prepositions that should be used after particular words and common errors of composition.

But before studying such matters it will be well to classify letters according to their purpose, and to form some general rules about arrangement and style.

There are three main classes of letter: Personal; Official; and Business. All letters can be placed in one of these classes.

Personal letters may be either informal or formal. Informal personal letters are those that are exchanged by relatives or friends. Such a letter may be a gossipy one, full of family news, descriptions of a holiday, a wedding, a party, a funeral.

It may be a love letter, or a letter of good wishes; it may offer thanks for a present, or a holiday visit. It may be from a boy at school asking for pocket money, or from a sailor describing a foreign port to his parents or girl friend.

Formal personal letters are those that have a more definite purpose, such as the acceptance or refusal of an invitation to a party or a wedding; congratulations to a friend on passing an examination, or obtaining a new job, or becoming engaged; or sympathy with an office colleague who has suffered a bereavement.

Official letters are those exchanged by a private person and a civil servant, local government official, employer, Member of Parliament or other person or body having an official position. Letters between landlord and tenant, between ratepayer and town clerk, between householder and electricity board come into this class. So do letters between a taxpayer and the Inland Revenue Department; letters written to a company, applying for employment, and by an employer giving a reference to a departing employee; in fact all correspondence involving a private individual and an official matter.

Finally, business letters are, obviously, those exchanged between one business man or company and another. They may contain orders, or refer to the receipt of orders. They may deal with legal matters: contracts, wills, summonses, affecting a business; or with an architect's plans for the construction of a building, and the orders for materials, and their delivery to the site.

Certain principles apply to letters of all classes. The first of these is the observance of the ordinary rules of good conduct: truth and honesty, courtesy and tact, are as important in a letter as they are in everything else, even when you are writing a letter of complaint or remonstrance.

Sincerity and simplicity are other qualities which should be made manifest in every letter, but especially in personal letters. Your letter expresses *yourself*, as if you were talking to the reader of it, and the sincerity, the naturalness and the intimacy of conversation must be conveyed. Consequently, any kind of formality or pomposity is entirely out of place; and although it is possible to overdo the conversational style and lower the tone of the letter it is essential to avoid being starchy or patronising.

Next, it is essential to write in an appropriate style. You

would not write in love letter style to the managing director of a company to whom you are applying for employment. A letter from an aunt to her favourite nephew would be written in a different manner from that of a bank manager to a client who has overdrawn his account. You must take care that not only what you write, but the way you write it, will not give offence, shock, misinformation or a false impression to the reader.

Lastly, there is the appearance of a letter. Bad handwriting or blotted and straggling lines may completely spoil the recipient's pleasure. Errors in spelling, or typing, or forms of addressing people, bad spacing, irregular alignment, or mistakes in facts or figures in a business letter, may cause serious loss to the writer or to his employers.

No matter what kind of letter you may be writing, make sure that it looks clean and neat, thus showing that you have taken trouble with its production.

It is convenient to divide a letter—any letter—into its components, and then see how they should be arranged. There are ten parts of a letter:

> address
> date
> direction
> salutation (or greeting)
> reference (or heading)
> body
> subscription (or closing phrase)
> signature
> postscript (if any)
> the envelope

The ADDRESS is, of course, the sender's address. Letters sent from offices on business matters always have printed headings at the top of the sheet. This address includes the name and address of the company, the department of central government or local government, or the other official body from which the letter is going out.

On a private letter your address should appear in the top right-hand corner, arranged so that it can be read easily. The arrangement of the lines may be either straight or staggered according to your own ideas and the nature of your address; but there must be separate lines. The first will be the name, if any, of your house. The second will be the number of your house and the name of the road. The third will be the village, town or city; then the county, and last, your Postcode (if any). For example:

> Brownstones,
>   17 Scarlet Street,
>   Greyling,
>   Cheshire.

or :

> Brownstones,
> 17 Scarlet Street,
> Greyling,
> Cheshire.

There are recognised contractions for many of the counties in the British Isles (see page 152) and these may be used on envelopes; but it is better to use the county's name in full when writing your own address. More will be said about addresses and counties when we consider the envelope.

Though the address on your letters may be either hand-written or typed, a much better effect is achieved by having your writing paper die-stamped. Most good class stationers will show you samples of lettering and arrangement, and engrave a die to your order. This costs from 8/6 for 12 letters, and a few pence for each extra letter in the address. Once the die is made the only cost in future is the actual die-stamping on the paper. This is usually from 13/- for 100 sheets (one pad), but if you have 200 or more sheets done at once it only costs about 2/- for each 100 sheets after the first. The die is kept by the stationer ready for when you re-order.

It is usually best to use single sheets of paper (which will be bound back into a pad after die-stamping if you wish), as a plain matching sheet can then be used for a second page. When choosing the style of your address, bear your own hand-writing in mind. If it is bold and heavy it can easily make small lettering look insignificant. The colour you choose will depend mainly on the colour of the paper, but black or blue are almost always the most satisfactory.

Another method of putting the address at the head of your letters is by means of an embossing press. This is a stamp bearing your address in metal characters which makes a raised impression on the paper. The cost of the press, complete with an address and telephone number is from 47/6. An extra charge is made for additional words.

Private notepaper may have your address *printed* on it; but it is best to have a plate engraved with address, telephone number and (if you have any) your title and decorations as they should appear on a letter sent *to* you.

The next part of your letter is the DATE. That looks a simple matter, but it is surprising how many people either forget to date their letters at all, or just scribble 'Monday' under the address.

There are many ways of writing a date. Examples are:

October 9, 1961	Oct. 9, 1961
9th October, 1961	9th Oct., 1961
October 9th, 1961	Oct. 9th, 1961

We never write 'October the 9th' or 'The 9th of October'. Some people prefer to write only the figures; and then it is usual (in England, but not in some foreign countries) to put the number of the month in the middle, thus: 9.10.61. or 9.x.61. This should never be done on a formal, official or commercial letter; and on those letters it is better to write the name of the month in full, not in contracted form. Americans reverse the order of the figures for month and day, making October 9th read 10.9.61.

Next comes the DIRECTION. By this is meant the name and the address of the person or company to whom you are writing. Of course you do not need to put a Direction at all if you are writing to Mother, or Uncle Bill; but it is essential if your letter is written on business of any kind.

There should be a margin of half an inch or an inch on the left side of each page of every letter—except, perhaps, the purely personal letter. But formal, official and business letters should always have a good-sized margin so that they can be filed easily. It is always wise to keep a copy of every official or business letter for reference, or simply to prove that it was in fact written.

The Direction should be written close to the left hand margin, then, beginning a line below the line of the date. It may, like the Address, be either 'straight' or 'staggered', but in any case it should be in exactly the same form as the address on the envelope.

Sometimes the Direction is put not at the top left side of the letter, but at the foot of the letter on the left, beginning a line below the signature. This may be done when the letter, although of a personal nature, is of a formal kind; or is sent to someone of higher social standing than yourself; or is of an informal nature but is addressed to someone at his office address instead of his home.

The wording of the Direction will depend, of course, on circumstances. To a private individual you will address your letter:

	J. J. Jones, Esq.,
to a woman:	Miss J. J. Jones,
or	Mrs J. J. Jones;

but if the person to whom you are writing has a title, or a right to any special designation of rank or office, the rules are somewhat complicated. They will be found in Section 3 of this book.

If you are writing to an unlimited company, or a partnership of traders or solicitors, or any firm that is not styled 'limited', the Direction should be

	Messrs Jones and Company,
or	Messrs Jones and Partners,
or	Messrs Jones, Smith & Brown,

or whatever the designation may be. 'Messrs' is the plural form of 'Mister' (contracted to 'Mr') and is itself a contraction of the French word *Messieurs*, the plural of *Monsieur* (which means Mister).

But in the case of a limited company, where the word 'Limited' is part of the designation, you should *not* put 'Messrs' before its name. The idea is that a limited company is almost always an association of many shareholders or stockholders; not, as is an unlimited company or a firm of solicitors, a partnership of two or three individual partners who can properly be addressed as 'Messrs'. Consequently, it is usually best to address your letter to some individual—The Managing Director, The Personnel Manager, The Secretary, The Branch Manager, The Export Manager—followed by the name of the company, thus:

The Branch Manager,
Central Bank Ltd,
222 Middling Street,
London, E.C.4.

or   The Personnel Manager,
          The Iceberg Manufacturing Co., Ltd,
             260 South India Street,
                Liverpool 97.

This enables you to write with more sense of being in personal contact with somebody than if you simply address your letter to an impersonal entity.

The additional letters and figures allocated to each of the 20 million postal addresses in the UK (called Postcoding; introduced between 1968 and 1971) should be clearly written, typed or printed after the name of the town or the country on your letter-heading and on the envelope. It should be the last item of the address.

Next follows the SALUTATION or GREETING. This comes immediately under the Direction, with a blank line left in between, and is usually set close up to the left-hand margin. Most forms of salutation begin with 'Dear', no matter whether you have affection, hatred, indifference or contempt for the person you are addressing. It is a long-established convention that everyone to whom you write is 'Dear' to you. The word is only omitted in the case of strictly formal letters to or from Government departments or officials, when a plain

Sir, *or* Madam,

is usual; in the case of a letter to a woman whom you do not know personally, when

Dear Madam

is the usual form (or, very formally, Madam); and in the case of certain persons with titles or official designations (these are dealt with later).

Apart from these exceptions, the usual form of salutation to any correspondent other than a relative or intimate friend is

Dear Sir,

and this is the form most generally used in business correspondence. If the Direction of your letters is to Messrs
Smith & Company, you would begin

> 'Dear Sirs',
> *or, more formally,*   'Gentlemen'.

Also, use 'Dear Sirs' when addressing an unlimited company or a partnership; 'Gentlemen' to a limited company (see
page 18).

This last style ('Gentlemen') is best used when you wish to
show a special measure of respect, as when a clerk or a
manager writes to his Board of Directors. It is also suitable
when beginning a report or a submission of a claim or a
complaint to a committee, public body or local authority.

If the person to whom you are writing is someone with
whom you wish to establish the 'personal touch' in business
relations, you will begin:

> Dear Mr Brown,
> Dear Brown,
> *or*   My Dear Mr Brown,
> My Dear Brown,

the 'My' adding an extra measure of intimacy, cordiality or
liking to the 'Dear Brown' form.

But you need to be careful with the 'My' forms, because the
'My' *may* be thought to be patronising, or even insulting.
Sometimes a letter to someone with whom you are not quite
on 'Mr Smith' terms may be begun with 'My Dear Sir' instead
of the ordinary 'Dear Sir', but there again care and tact should
be used in deciding whether to use the form or not.

If you choose to begin your letter with the Salutation

> 'Gentlemen',

use the word in full. Do *not* contract it to 'Gents'. In fact,
contractions anywhere in a letter should be avoided, as giving
a suggestion of your being in too much of a hurry to write the
word in full. The only exceptions are 'Co', or 'Coy' for
'Company' and 'Ltd' for 'Limited'. (For punctuation, see
pages 136–138.)

The BODY of the letter will begin just to the right of, and
below, the end of the salutation; or, if the salutation is a long

one, begin somewhere near its right. If you are writing your letter by hand, begin your letter on the next line below the Salutation; if you are typing it, leave one clear blank line between the salutation and the line on which the body of the letter begins.

22 Egbert Street,
Alfred-on-Tyne,
Northumberland.
June 30, 1959.

John Smith, Esq.,
5A Cummerbund Street,
Bath.

Dear Mr Smith,
Thank you for your letter of June 25th. . . .

But if, instead of 'John Smith', your correspondent has a long name, such as 'Roderick Stephenson', you might begin your letter:

Dear Mr Stephenson,
Thank you for your letter of . . .

which saves you from having to begin each paragraph in the middle of the page, or nearly so. For wherever you start the first paragraph of your letter, every other paragraph must start directly below it to give a tidy appearance to the page.

It is a fairly general practice in writing professional or commercial letters to put a HEADING above the Body, stating the subject of the letter (provided that the letter deals with only one subject) or the reference number of the letter to which yours is a reply.

John Smith, Esq.,
5A Cummerbund Street,
Bath.

Dear Mr Smith,

Sale of farm

Thank you for your letter of June 25th. My farm is still for sale, as advertised in *The Farm Gazette* for June 24. . . .

Some business houses have spaces for references, usually placed above the Direction, so that letters may easily be found in the files. *Eg*,

Our ref. . . .
Your ref. . . .

with some arrangement of letters and figures; or letters or figures only which sometimes include the year, and sometimes are broken up by oblique strokes. Or the reference may consist of the initials of the member of the firm who dictated the letter, so that the reply can be handed to him when the incoming mail is sorted. Sometimes the initials of the typist who typed the letter are included in the reference.

Where a subject heading is used, you will sometimes see the word 'Re' put in front of it; *eg*,

Re Sale of farm.

This is quite wrong. Many people think that 're' means 'about' but it does not. It is, in fact, a part of the Latin word *res*, which means thing, object, affair, matters, circumstance, state. It is used by lawyers for the title of a lawsuit, which they style '*In re* John Doe deceased', for example; by which they mean '*In the matter of* the late John Doe'.

The same ruling applies to those stupid contractions for the months which were commonly used at one time: *inst.*, *ult.* and *prox.* They have largely died out, but are still used by some old-fashioned people. They mean, respectively, the present month, last month, and next month; but why not use the actual date? Nothing is gained by writing 'Thank you for your letter of the 6th ult.', instead of 'Thank you for your letter of May 6th'.

The body of your letter should be arranged in paragraphs. The beginning of the first paragraph will be below and to the right of the end of the Salutation (*ie*, 'indented' several spaces from the right-hand side of the margin on the left of the sheet) and every succeeding paragraph will have its beginning directly below that of the first. The paragraphing is more important in a business letter than it is in a personal letter; but even there it helps to give your letter a good appearance and to make it more easily readable.

If your letter deals with several different subjects each should be given a fresh paragraph. If you must deal with a subject at considerable length, use two or more paragraphs. By breaking up a page your reader will more easily follow your argument or grasp your subject.

In a commercial letter which is concerned with a number of orders for different articles or materials, or with a number of different customers, each point should be contained in a separate paragraph. This makes it easier for the orders to be understood, and it also facilitates checking when they are being made up, or the details are being distributed to different departments for attention.

In some branches of the Armed Forces it is a rule in correspondence that each paragraph shall be numbered. The number is placed at the edge of the left hand margin of the page, so that it stands out from the body of the paragraph because of the 'indenting' of the first line of each paragraph. Thus:

Sir,

1. I acknowledge with thanks your letter of . . .
2. The construction of the brick buildings to which you refer has been in progress since April 16th 1968, and completion is expected by December 31st 1968.
3. Materials for the construction of the timber buildings which was the subject of your letter dated . . .

The great value of numbering each paragraph is that in a reply to the letter, or in any further letter, exact reference can be made to any subject dealt with by simply writing: 'Referring to paragraph 4 of my letter dated July 3rd 1969 . . .'

In most letters the introductory paragraph is specially important because it draws the reader's attention to previous correspondence, or to the main purpose of the present letter. The most frequent beginning of a commercial or professional letter is: 'In reply to your letter of June 5th', or 'Thank you for your letter of June 5th', or 'Further to my letter of June 5th'. If you are writing in reply to an advertisement—employment, a house, goods for sale—you will probably begin: 'Referring to your advertisement in the *Daily* —— dated June 5th', or 'In response to your advertisement . . .' or 'Please send me so-and-so, as advertised in the *Daily* —— dated June 5th'.

In a long letter, dealing with an important matter, try to set out your points in a way that is both logical and chronological. You must marshal your argument in an orderly way, reduce

it to the right order of the occurrence of events or the development of your case, and then use simple, telling sentences,
grouped into short and concise paragraphs, to press home
your points. A well-planned argument, set out neatly in well-
arranged paragraphs, stands a better chance of succeeding
than a slovenly letter which is difficult to understand and
looks as if the writer had given no real thought to what he
was writing.

A word to avoid is *beg*, especially in such phrases as 'I beg
to acknowledge receipt of your letter . . .' or 'I beg to apply
for the position advertised . . .' Nobody is a *beggar* nowadays
and there is no need to put yourself into the position of
appearing to be a very humble suppliant for favours. The
word is used rightly enough in the phrase 'I beg to differ
from you' which is a polite way of saying 'You're a liar!'
The full form is, or was, 'I beg your leave to differ', which is
somewhat out-of-date now, but is sometimes heard in public
debates where contestants are anxious to keep their tempers
and be polite, and in the House of Commons where the word
'liar' is out of order.

Also out of fashion are those flowery, artificial phrases that
used to adorn business and professional letters, and make
them appear (to our eyes) insincere and unrealistic. Examples
(to be avoided) are:

Your esteemed favour to hand . . .

Thanking you in anticipation of future favours . . .

Our Mr Jones will be at the disposal of your goodself on
Wednesday next.

Enclosed please find our list of prices current.

We are in receipt of your communication of even date and
beg to thank you for same.

A letter, even one with a large order in it, is not an 'esteemed
favour', and such exaggeration in language does credit
neither to its writer nor the recipient. The craving for more
orders expressed in the second example is unworthy; if your
goods are suitable, the further orders will come, so why go
on your knees for them? 'Our Mr Jones' unnecessarily
patronises Mr Jones; the 'Our' should be omitted. 'Your
goodself' is sheer nonsense, of course; it was once intended

to be either courtesy or flattery, but it has no place in modern parlance. 'I enclose' is better than 'Enclosed please find'—your correspondent will surely have no difficulty in locating the price list in the envelope. For the last example substitute 'Thank you for your letter of today's date'.

Unfortunately, many of these tricks of writing, pomposities and meaningless phrases—especially those used in the next part of a letter, the subscription—became stereotyped many years ago, and have been repeated in successive textbooks on commercial correspondence. However, the more realistic and sincere style suited to modern times is increasingly used.

After the Body, the next part of a letter is the SUBSCRIPTION. This word comes from two Latin words which mean 'written underneath'. It is applied to the phrase or phrases, of a complimentary or formal character, with which your letter ends (apart from your signature). The most commonly used is

> Yours faithfully,

and others are

> Yours truly,
> Yours very truly,
> Yours respectfully,
> Your obedient servant.

Sometimes it is fitting to put, before one of these phrases,

> I am,
> I remain,
> We remain,
> I am, Sir (*or* I am, Dear Sir),
> We remain, Gentlemen.

The most general subscription is 'Yours faithfully'. Somewhat warmer than that is 'Yours truly'. Still more cordial and friendly is 'Yours sincerely'. All of these may be used in personal letters, formal or informal, as well as in many kinds of professional and commercial letters. For the more intimate personal letters there is a wide choice among—

> Yours affectionately
> Very sincerely yours
> Your affectionate
> Yours ever

and many variations of these phrases.

It should be noted that a capital letter is needed for the first word of each line of the subscription; that each phrase begins on a fresh line; and that 'Yours' needs no apostrophe (Your's is wrong).

An important point to observe in ending a letter is to make the Subscription tally with the Salutation and the Body. For example, if the letter begins 'Dear Sirs' it should end with 'We are, Dear Sirs', and if it begins 'Gentlemen' it should end with 'We are, Gentlemen', &c. Likewise, if in the Body you write in first person singular style—'I shall be glad to send you the book mentioned in your letter'—do not end with '*We* are', &c. Write 'I am, Yours faithfully'.

If you are applying for a job (Section 2 of this book deals with this kind of letter) there is no need to end your letter with 'Your obedient servant' or 'Yours obediently'. Until you are engaged, you are not the obedient servant of the person or company concerned. 'Yours faithfully' is adequate. 'Your obedient servant' is sometimes used in official correspondence, and sometimes in letters to the editor of a newspaper—a traditional ending, which has nearly died out.

A letter that is in the form of a report by a departmental head to his superior (general manager, director, board) may properly be subscribed 'Yours respectfully'. So also may a letter from an employee to a superior in which the employee submits a statement on some aspect of his work; expresses thanks for a commendation or an increase of salary; applies for an increase of salary; or gives notice of his intention to leave his employment.

After the Subscription comes the SIGNATURE. A personal letter will be signed in the manner in which you are usually known to the recipient: John, Uncle Bill, Mother, A. J., Auntie. You may like to sign your letter with a nickname that is well known to the friend or relative to whom you are writing. There is one suggestion about that, however, which may save you some embarrassment. If you sign with a nickname, write your proper name above the address. Then, if the addressee happens to have moved without leaving a forwarding address, and the letter has to be opened and returned to you by the Post Office, you will not blush when you think of how many people may have chuckled to see a letter marked *Opened and Officially Sealed* and addressed to 'Coppernob' or 'Popsie' at your home address!

The signature on a more formal personal letter will generally be more like the personal signature on a business letter; *ie*, your initials and surname, or the form of signature which you have chosen for a business signature. This may be in any form you choose:

> John B. Smith
> J. Burslem Smith
> J. B. Smith
> John B. C. Smith
> John B. Chas. Smith
> Jack Smith

If you hold some special position in your company, or club, or a military rank which you are authorised to use and your letter is connected with the affairs of the company, club, society, military or ex-service body or committee in which you hold a position, it is customarily typed or written below your signature. For example:

> On behalf of the Committee,
> John Smith
> Hon. Secretary.

or, on headed notepaper,

> Yours faithfully,
> John Smith.
> (President)

or
> Yours very truly
> J. B. Smith.
> Lt-Col (retd)

or
> Your obedient servant,
> J. B. Smith.
> Captain, RN
> Commanding HM Ship *Optic*

But the armed services have their own rules and practices in respect of letter writing and signatures, into which it is unnecessary to enter in this book.

If you have developed a signature which you have found from experience to be difficult to read, it is always helpful to type or print it underneath your actual signature.

Women who sign letters with their initials and surname

only and then reproach other people for writing back to them as 'Mr' have only themselves to blame. They often cause confusion and annoyance by omitting to indicate their sex when they sign their letters; and not only their sex, but their marital status too. A woman signing a letter to a stranger should make clear who and what she is, and this can be done in several ways.

She should use one of her given names in her signature: *eg*,

> Yours sincerely,
> Eileen Waters.

Then she should state plainly whether she is married or single, thus:

> Yours sincerely,
> (Miss) Eileen Waters.

If she is married, the correct way to address a letter to her is by her husband's given name or initials, not her own. So a married woman should have her correct style typed underneath her signature, thus:

> Yours sincerely,
> Eileen Waters.
> (Mrs. R. J. Waters).

She may, of course, have some other form of signature, but, whatever it is, it should make clear those points: that she is a woman, whether she is married, and what style should be used in addressing a reply to her. She may like to sign as 'Margaret J. Eileen Waters' but it is still necessary to prefix '(Miss)' or to subscribe '(Mrs. R. J. Waters)' if misunderstandings are to be avoided.

A baronet or a knight sometimes has his name and title on his notepaper in the top left corner; *eg*,

> From Sir John Smith, KBE

so that strangers to whom he has occasion to write may know which 'John Smith' the letter comes from, and the correct style of addressing a reply to his letter.

Signatures on commercial letters depend on circumstances. Obviously, a letter cannot be signed by a limited company; it must be signed by a person, on behalf of the company. The practice adopted varies according to the wishes of the board of directors, or the proprietor or partners, or the managing director or the secretary.

A letter for which a departmental chief is responsible may be signed

> Yours faithfully,
> John Smith.
> Sales Manager.

or 'Secretary' or 'Branch Manager' or 'Managing Director' or whatever position of responsibility the writer may hold.

Another method, if the letter is coming from a company, is to sign:

> We are, Gentlemen,
> Yours faithfully,
> THE BROWN BOOT COMPANY LIMITED
> John Smith.
> Secretary.

Or the word 'For' may be placed in front of the company's name. Sometimes, in very formal letters or reports, this is elaborated into:

> Yours faithfully,
> (For and on behalf of)
> BROWN, JONES & BOOT, Ltd.
> John Smith.
> Managing Director.

In large organisations it is impossible for the head of the business to sign all the correspondence personally, although many of the letters may have to go out over his name, and he will accept responsibility for them. Whether his signature is typed on the letter or a rubber stamp of it is used, there should be an actual signature of some person who is authorised to sign in his name, or to use his rubber stamp. Also, although a business chief may usually sign all his letters personally, there are times when he has to rush off (to a conference, a golf course, or his wife) before they are all ready for signing.

Some people use, in these circumstances, the *per pro* method; and quite often use it incorrectly. *Per pro* is a contraction of two Latin words, *per procurationem*, and they mean 'by the agency of'. They may even be further contracted into *pp.* The correct way of using this contraction is shown in the following example:

> Yours faithfully,
> John Smith.
> Managing Director.
> per pro: W. Brown.

or   We are, Sir,
> Yours respectfully,
> Long & Burton Ltd.
> (pp. C. Jones)

The mistake that is sometimes made is to place the *per pro:* before the name of the company, or the managing director for whom his private secretary is signing, as if *per pro:* meant 'on behalf of' or 'for', instead of 'by the agency of'. It is WRONG to sign

> Yours faithfully,
> per pro: OXFORDS LIMITED.
> J. Smith.

In large industrial companies, head offices of banks, Government and local government departments and large partnerships (solicitors, estate agents) it is necessary to be careful about authorising the signing of letters, and to restrict this power to a small number of responsible people. Otherwise letters might go forth in the name of the company, department or partnership containing errors for which the company would be liable.

The right to sign for the firm, either with a signature followed by a statement of the writer's position (secretary, director, manager) or with the firm's or department's name and a *per pro:* signature, is usually customary, a practice that has been exercised over many years and is fully recognised by all concerned; or authority is specifically given to certain persons. In some cases, a legal instrument called a Power of Attorney is executed, authorising one or more named persons to sign letters, with or without the *per pro:* form.

There is one, and only one, kind of letter that requires no signature at all; that is the 'third person' letter, the formal acceptance or refusal, expression of thanks or sympathy. (This is dealt with on pages 101–104.)

The ninth part of a letter is the POSTSCRIPT—if any. It is best to do without one, but sometimes a thought occurs after the letter is signed, or some item of information only then becomes known to the writer, and a Postscript, or PS, becomes unavoidable. The word is a shortened form of the Latin *postscriptum*, and simply means something 'written after' the rest.

If a second thought occurs to you after you have written a PS, there is no need to write 'PS2'. Both your postscripts have been 'written after' the letter was ended, and it is unnecessary to number them. The full stops are unnecessary, too. Some letter writers like to save up a particular point to put into a PS, with the idea that it is a good thing to put 'a sting in the tail' of their letter, where it will be more heavily impressed on the reader's mind.

Finally, we must consider the ENVELOPE. The addressing of it should be perfectly clear, for the benefit of the Post Office; and it should be designed to create a good impression on the recipient before he opens it. This second object is achieved by the neatness of the writing or typing of the address.

The first point to consider is, where to begin. Remembering that all letters are sorted and faced one way and then run through a machine which cancels the stamp with a 'postmark', it is obvious that the stamp must be stuck in the top right corner, and that the address should start well below the level of the stamp, so that it will not be obscured by the postmark. Then, to allow for long words in the address, it should be begun well over towards the left side of the envelope.

In the British Isles, and generally in the Commonwealth, it is customary to write, as separate lines, first the name of the person to whom the letter is addressed; then the number of the building and the name of the street or road; then the town, or city with any special designation of postal district (*eg*, EC4, C6 or 20 or the postal code see page 19); and finally, the name of the county—followed by the name of the country, if the letter is being sent abroad. For example:

Mr John Smith,
2 Brown Street,
Greenside,
Cheshire.

or   John P. Brown, Esq.,
                        2 Green Street,
                        Brownside,
                        Queensland,
                        Australia.

In some countries, however, it is customary to place the
street number *after* the name of the street; *eg*,

                    M. J. Dupont,
                    rue Royale 17,
                    Rouen,
                    France.

and in some countries it is customary to write the name of the
state or province or town first, and the name of the street
below it, on the principle that in sorting letters, the routeing is
first to the province, then to the town and lastly to the street
and the number in that street. This may be logical and
orderly; but the British are neither. However, when writing
a letter to a correspondent abroad it is sensible, as well as
courteous, to conform to his methods, and to write for
example:

                    Herrn G. Braun,
                    22c Bonn/Rhein,
                    Hannover strasse 699,
                    Germany.

The name of the country is placed last, for the benefit of
English postal sorters. Apart from that, the city and province
come first after the name, and then the name of the street, and
the number of the house.

Whether, in letters to British people of masculine sex, you
should write 'Mr' or 'Esq.' is a matter of individual choice and
feeling. The only certain rules are that one or the other must
be used (provided that he has no particular rank or title); and
that both must never be used. (It is *wrong* to write 'Mr John
Smith, Esq.') (See also page 39.)

The practice of writing

                    John Smith, Esq.,

and designating every man an Esquire is comparatively
modern, is to the purist usually wrong, and is entirely harm-

less. Strictly speaking, the purists say, the word belongs to a
certain class only, and they call in history to their support,
reminding us that esquires were youths of noble birth who
attended on armoured knights and nobles, and aspired to be
knights or nobles themselves in due course.

Therefore, they say, only untitled 'men of property' can be
styled Esq., and only the head of a family can be styled an
Esq., and some assert that only the head of a family to whom
has been granted the right to bear a coat of arms can be styled
an Esq. For manual workers and shopkeepers, authors and
artists and farmers, the purists say, plain 'Mr' is enough. It is
even considered, in some circles, rude to address an envelope
to anyone above the rank of manual worker as 'Mr J. Smith'.

The addressing of a letter to a child is straightforward.
Up to the age of seven or so it may be enclosed inside a letter
to the parents.

From about seven onwards the letter should be fully
addressed, to 'Miss Jane Smith' or 'Master John Smith' at the
full home address, even though it may still be enclosed in a
letter to a parent. The style of 'Master' is the form of address
for the young boy; by the time he is twelve he should be
addressed simply by his full name without any prefix. When
he is in his mid-teens he becomes 'Mr' like his father.

All girls are 'Miss' on envelopes from about seven years
old onwards, until they marry, but it is as well to preserve the
convention about the way of differentiating among sisters.
The convention is that the first-born girl alone is entitled to
be addressed, in correspondence, as 'Miss Smith'. Her
younger sisters are known and addressed by their first names,
as 'Miss Jane Smith' and 'Miss Mary Smith' and so on. The
eldest, as long as she remains unmarried, is *the* 'Miss Smith' of
the family. When she marries and changes her name, her
next unmarried sister becomes 'Miss Smith'.

On marriage a woman (in British countries) loses her own
surname, which is called her 'maiden name', and hence-
forward uses that of her husband.

Exceptions to this general practice are women who have
become prominent in one of the professions or arts under
their maiden name, or under an adopted name, and do not
wish to lose its commercial or prestige value.

If you do not know a woman writer or actress personally
but you wish to write to her, you will address her by her

professional name and direct the letter to her publisher's offices or her theatre, or you may find her home address in reference books. Her married name may be there, too; but you should not use it unless you know her.

The practice in America is, often, for a woman to retain her maiden name after marriage as a middle name but usually without hyphening it to her new surname. Thus, Miss Jane Brown marries Mr John Maclean, and then styles herself 'Mrs Jane Brown Maclean'. This, in full, should be written on the envelope.

Other customs about names and signatures are followed in other countries. If you know them, follow them. If you do not, follow British customs, but be courteous. No one will worry about an error, provided that it is obviously unintentional.

Normally, however, in most British countries, a married woman is addressed in writing by her husband's name and his initials, or forename. If Miss Ada Brown marries Mr John Edward Smith, letters to her in future must be addressed to

Mrs J. E. Smith,
or   Mrs John Smith

or by whatever form the husband wishes to be known. She is *not* 'Mrs Ada Smith' or 'Mrs A. Smith' as long as her husband is alive.

But if she becomes a widow, or is legally separated from her husband, she may choose how she wishes to be addressed. She may continue to be styled

Mrs John Smith
or   Mrs J. E. Smith

or she may prefer to be Mrs A. Smith

or   Mrs Ada Smith

or even to revert to her pre-marriage name, especially if she had been previously married, or had borne a title acquired either by birth or by a previous marriage.

The forms of address for women of title are dealt with in Section 3.

The punctuation of the address on an envelope needs little comment. It is generally the same as the punctuation of the address, and the direction, in the letter itself. It is usual to end with a comma each line except the last, which has a full-stop, but none of these punctuation marks is really necessary. There is no need whatever to put (as many people do) the name of the house within quotation marks. A name is a name, and does not need quoting, as if it were a pretended name.

There is no need to put a comma after the number of the house, nor is it necessary to write 'No.' before the number.

In writing a name, put a fullstop after each initial. If the addressee is a man, put a comma after his surname, and if you are adding 'Esq.' follow that contraction with a fullstop and a comma. There is no need to put a fullstop after the contractions 'Mr' or 'Mrs' because they end with the same letter as that which ends the full word of which they are contracted forms: 'Mister' and 'Mistress'. A fullstop is needed, however, where the last letter of the full word is not the same as the last letter of the contraction: eg, 'Capt.' for 'Captain'—'Maj.-Gen.' for 'Major-General' and so forth. But on an envelope it is more polite to write these designations in full.

Here are some examples of (imaginary) addresses on envelopes:

> J. B. Jones, Esq.,
>   Flat 3,
>   Princess Court,
>   99 Midwinter Hill,
>   Hampstead,
>   London, NW3

> Mrs John Williams,
>   Ford Cottage,
>   Church Lane,
>   Whittingham,
>   Oxford.

> The Misses Smith,
>   678 Back Lane,
>   Glasgow, C4

Mr A. B. Charles,   Mr B. C. Robinson,
P.O. Box 5555,   15 Fosse Road,
Pretoria,   Cheam,
Transvaal,   Surrey.
South Africa.

If your letter contains private things which you would not wish any third party to read who might happen to open your letter, write

	Private
or	Personal
or	For personal attention

on the envelope; the best place is usually just above and slightly to the left of the name of the person to whom it is addressed. Or it may be put in the bottom left corner, below all the address, where it will not be obscured by the postmark.

This applies in particular to letters of a private character addressed to someone at a business address, where the morning's mail may all be opened and sorted by clerks or by a secretary. Letters so marked should, of course, not be opened by anyone but the addressee himself. If a personal letter is accidentally opened by someone else, it should be replaced in its envelope, which should be reclosed with gum or a gummed label, and marked 'opened in error' and initialled. Then it should be reposted or personally delivered to the addressee, and apology and explanation offered.

One other possibility needs sometimes to be provided for, when addressing a letter; that is the absence of the addressee from the address. If you have any grounds for thinking that the person to whom you are writing may have left the address temporarily or permanently, you should write directions on the envelope regarding its disposal. These may be written either in the bottom left corner, below the address, or on the back of the envelope. You may put:

	Please forward
or	If away, please forward
or	If undelivered, please return to

followed by your own name and address. Anyone who receives a letter so marked, when the addressee has indeed gone away, is in honour bound to deal with it as best he can in accordance with the sender's wishes.

If the new address is known, that on the envelope should be crossed through and the new address written alongside the old, leaving the addressee's name, of course, clearly legible. Then the letter should be posted in the usual way, and the Post Office will deliver it free to the new address.

If the new address is *not* known, and the sender's name and address appear on the back of the envelope with or without a specific request for the letter's return, the whole of the name and address on the front of the envelope should be crossed through, and the letters PTO (for 'Please turn over') should be written on it. The sender's name and address on the back should be underlined, or ringed, and the letter posted. The Post Office will return it to the sender, usually without any extra charge.

If the new address is unknown, and the sender has *not* put his own name and address on the back, the address on the front should be crossed through, the words 'Not known at this address' written alongside it, and the letter posted. It will then go to the Post Office department which deals with such cases. That department alone may open the letter to discover the sender's name and address; no private person has any right to do so. The department will then stick down the envelope with an official label on which the sender's name and address have been written, and send it back to him, with a note of the reason for its non-delivery to the original addressee. Fresh postage may be charged.

When stamping a letter, always be sure that you affix the correct value in stamps. If you have any doubt about what the postage is, ask at a Post Office. If insufficient stamps are put on a letter, the addressee will be charged double the amount of the difference between the correct postage and the value of the stamps actually used.

Finally, on these matters of writing and addressing and stamping letters, there is one other point that needs care. If you are writing several letters in succession, be sure to put the right letters in the right envelopes. Many people address the envelope first, put it to one side of the desk while they write the letter, and go on to write another envelope and another letter. It is fatally easy then to fold both letters and slip them into the envelopes without making certain that you have matched the letters to the right envelopes.

The British Post Office, which handles more than ten thousand million (10,000,000,000) letters and parcels every year, is experienced in delivering badly written, wrongly addressed and carelessly packed parcels of all shapes and sizes; but the *less* difficulty they have in dealing with each one of the cascade that pours into the sorting offices every day, the better chance they have of delivering *your* letter or parcel correctly and quickly. They suggest the following 11 points, care of which will help them to avoid delay to *your* mail.

1. Write or print the correct postal address very clearly on the envelope or parcel cover, including the Postcode.

2. Print the name of the POST TOWN in BLOCK LETTERS so that the sorter can read it quickly and accurately. (The post town is the town disposing of correspondence for a particular district. It may be some miles from the place of destination; it may even be in another county—*eg*, Long Eaton is in Derbyshire, but the post town for mails addressed to it is Nottingham. But the post town *must* appear in the address. It may be preceded by *via*.

3. Leave at least one and a half inches of space *above* the address.

4. Put the postage stamp in the top right-hand corner of the envelope.

5. Keep matter which has nothing to do with the address, such as reference numbers or advertisement, well away on the left-hand side.

6. Use house numbers, *not* names, whenever possible.

7. For parcels, see that the address is written on the actual wrapping paper. Do not rely on a tie-on label; and see that stick-on labels are stuck on securely.

8. Do *not* use 'Local' or 'By' or 'Near' or a telephone number in the address.

9. Do *not* use initials for places, such as 'N.B.' for Scotland (which might mean New Brunswick, Canada) or 'N.Z.' for New Zealand (which might be mistaken for London's N2 district); and do *not* use 'North Wales' (or 'N.W.') or 'South Wales' (or 'S.W.')—use the name of the county.

10. Write the county name in full unless it is one that has a recognised abbreviation, for example, 'Middx' for Middlesex. (See list page 152.)

11. Show your full postal address at the top of your note-paper, and in advertisements. (If in doubt about it, inquire at the local post office.)

It should be noted that London has many postal delivery areas, each with district initials and a number, which must be shown in the address. Letters and parcels posted in London for delivery in London need not have 'London' in the address, but they must have the initials and the number of the district.

Glasgow also has delivery areas with initials and numbers; and the following cities have district numbers without initials: Birmingham, Bradford, Brighton and Hove, Bristol, Edinburgh, Leeds, Liverpool, Manchester and Salford, Newcastle upon Tyne and Gateshead, and Sheffield. The district numbers are an essential part of the address. (See also Postcoding, page 19.)

WRITING MATERIALS

To create the best impression a letter must not only be well written but must also look attractive, and it is well worth giving some thought to the paper and ink you use. For personal letters, writing paper should be a pale blue or grey, white or cream, in one of the standard sizes of a good manufacturer. 'Deckle edge' paper is now out of fashion.

If your handwriting has a tendency to wander up or down as you go across the page do not use lined paper, but slip a piece of paper ruled with heavy black lines under the sheet on which you are writing. This will show through enough to help you to keep the writing straight.

The colour of the ink you use will depend on the colour of your paper and the die-stamped address, if you have one. Blue-black is the most usual and probably the best, but black or blue can also look well. Never use green, red or violet ink. Blue ink does not show up clearly on blue paper. Black is better.

The best shape and size of envelope for private correspondence in the 'Post Office Preferred' range is the one measuring 6 inches by $3\frac{1}{2}$ inches. A limited number of other shapes and sizes for business use are in the 'POP' range.

NO 'ESQ.' ABROAD

The contraction 'Esq.' (for 'Esquire') has no meaning or use in foreign countries (including the USA). So when you write to a friend on holiday or business abroad, address the envelope to 'Mr John Smith' and *not* 'John Smith, Esq.'. Most foreigners can translate 'Mr', but few know of 'Esq.'.

This caution applies especially to letters addressed 'Post Restante' at some town abroad, to be called for at the post office. Letters with address ending with 'Esq.' are likely to go into the E pigeon-hole.

YOUR JOB

PROBABLY THE most important, and most difficult, letters that people ever write are those in which the writer asks for employment. It may be that he, or she, is writing in quest of the first job after leaving school, university or the Armed Forces; or it may be the letter of a man or woman seeking a higher post, or one engaged on the nearly heartbreaking task of trying to end a period of unemployment.

So much in terms of human happiness may depend on the turn of a phrase, on the impression that is produced in the mind of a remote and quite unknown reader—the man or woman in whose hands one's fate may lie. At least, that is what the writer may often feel; but really it is not usually as tragic a matter as all that. There are always other openings, other employers.

Many large employers, such as the Government, the British Broadcasting Corporation and certain big firms, do not require a detailed letter in answer to an advertised post. It is only necessary to write asking for an application form. This form, often consisting of several pages of questions, needs to be completed carefully and truthfully, and returned promptly. On your answers will depend whether you are sent for to be interviewed.

There is, of course, no reason why you should not write an ordinary letter of application for employment to any of these employers, without waiting for them to advertise vacancies. The response, however, will generally be either a courteous note saying that there are no vacancies, or an application form for you to fill in. If you adopt this course—perhaps because you feel convinced that you would like a job in the organisation you have chosen—the following suggestions will apply equally to you.

Whether you write to a prospective employer in response to an advertisement or just 'out of the blue' certain essential considerations and probabilities must be borne in mind.

The first is that your letter will probably have to compete for attention with a large number of others. You may not realise just how great the competition usually is for the average run of non-specialist posts. One small advertisement offering a routine sort of £10-a-week job, inserted in one issue of a London evening paper at the time of writing these words, brought in more than 250 applications—some of them from entirely unsuitable people.

There is no need to be discouraged by the thought that hundreds of other people may also be applying for the position you want. But the knowledge should stimulate you to think very hard about your letter. You will, if you bear this probability in mind,

(1) plan your letter with care, so that it stands out from the rest;

(2) draft it roughly, putting in all the relevant facts you can think of;

(3) check that you have included all the essentials (of which more later), and kept out everything irrelevant;

(4) check that what you have written tallies with the details in the advertisement;

(5) write or type your letter neatly, clearly and in accordance with the accepted methods of arrangement and spacing;

(6) check it all again, and keep a copy for yourself;

(7) enclose a stamped addressed envelope (addressed to yourself) if you expect a reply;

(8) make sure the envelope is correctly addressed, as stated in the advertisement or in accordance with commonsense.

Some of these points may usefully be elaborated here. The first, to plan your letter so that it will stand out from the others, is obviously the most important thing to do, when you remember that your letter may be competing for attention with a great many others. If you cannot plan a letter, you are unlikely to be able to plan anything else. One large employer says that he takes more kindly to an application that is divided into two parts: one being wholly factual, giving brief chronological details; the other being concerned with applying for the post and 'selling' the applicant's personality. It is a question, he adds, of making him say to himself 'That is interesting, I'll read it again'.

You will find that the making of a draft, even of two or

three drafts, will help you to marshal all the items of information which can give weight to your application. In revising your draft you can strike out those that on consideration you feel do not further your cause; and perhaps other useful items will come into your head which could be added with advantage. You may also find that a different arrangement would be more effective.

It is extremely important that all the following facts should be included in every letter of application:

> your full name;
> full address;
> your age;
> whether married or single (and number of children, if any);
> if you are a woman, indicate your status by writing (Miss) or (Mrs) before your signature; and
> the position for which you are applying.

'Write or type your letter neatly'—but which shall it be? Apart from those advertisements which ask you to reply in your own handwriting, the answer depends partly on the quality of your handwriting (and your typing) and partly on the length of the letter.

Of course, if you are applying for a position as a typist or secretary, it is almost essential to type the letter.

In composing your letter one point should be emphasised strongly. Employers want the people they engage to be enthusiastic, to be interested in the firm and its activities; they want to be convinced by the applicant that he is anxious to work for that particular firm. If the letter betrays the fact that the writer does not know what the business of the company is, he is hardly likely to be engaged. With sincerity and truthfulness must march interest and enthusiasm, if one is not merely to get the job but to make progress in it.

Probably the most important of the components of a letter applying for a job may be set down thus:

> personality and character;
> knowledge and experience;
> composition and style.

The first of the three may not be expressed in words, yet it is expressed in the whole letter, 'between the lines'.

Remembering that if the letter is well received by the staff manager who reads it, the next step is likely to be either the arrival of a form to complete, or an invitation to come for an interview, the setting out of your knowledge and experience needs care. Nothing but the honest truth will do; every statement will probably be checked and referees will be asked for confidential estimates of you and details of their personal knowledge of you. You may also be required to show your birth certificate to prove your age (for purposes of superannuation) and you may be asked to undergo a medical examination.

As to how details of your knowledge and experience should be set forth, that depends on the details themselves, on the nature of the job you are applying for and on yourself. Some people favour a chronological form, covering every aspect of one's life from place of birth and education to previous service and present occupation. Others prefer a narrative method, descriptive of one's career in recent years, and then going back to mention one's education in general terms.

On these matters the views of several big employers (see page 9), or their staff managers, have been obtained. Mr A writes:

'On the question of setting out particulars of education, I do not feel that a tabulated style impresses more than a narrative style. Obviously a good narrative style stimulates interest.

'Age, obviously, is a question to be considered, and, while the majority of our openings are for men under forty, the personality that breaks through a well-written letter will often result in our seeing older men and fitting them in. In this group of companies we tend to look not necessarily at the age of the applicant, but more on the years yet to go before he is sixty-five; and when you look at it in that way, an applicant can well be considered at any age provided he is sufficiently versatile for his age not to have resulted in his being too set in his ways.'

It will be seen that Mr A stresses the importance of personality regardless of age, and shows that personality can 'break through' a letter. He indicates, too, that although an applicant may be over forty he may still stand a good chance of engagement, and therefore he should not try to minimise or conceal his age.

Mr B writes, referring to the need for enthusiasm on the part of the applicant:

'You try to look at a person through a sheet of paper, and the man who can show you that his experience has been accompanied by an enthusiasm for whatever he has done starts off with an advantage.

'It often strikes me as remarkable,' he goes on, 'that a man will apply for a post from another part of the country knowing nothing about the company to which he is going to link his future. The applicant who shows that he knows something about our company, even if it is only what he sees in the national advertising campaigns, starts off also with an advantage.

'The build-up is towards the fact that the applicant wants to work for this company above all others, and somehow he must avoid giving the impression that he has written a stereotyped sort of letter to half the companies that advertised that day in a particular daily newspaper. He may well have done so, but he must disguise the fact.'

Referring to the letter written by the professional letter writer, Mr B says:

'This is quite a serious development, and a considerable number of people lose a chance of ever being looked at by the fact that they go to a professional letter writer, whose methods are only too transparent to anyone who has to read numbers of them over the period of a year.'

Mr C, staff manager of another large organisation, writes:

'The type of letter which would persuade us to invite the writer to attend for an interview is one that is reasonably neat and legible and contains sufficient information concerning the writer's qualifications and background to indicate to us that he or she is probably the type of person we wish to employ.

'Letters which invariably prejudice an employer against an applicant from the outset are those which are written in a slovenly fashion. We receive a surprising number of these, and some of the worst offenders in this respect are senior pupils from schools, and university undergraduates, who do not seem to appreciate that an untidy letter containing mistakes and corrections is nothing more than a form of bad manners.

'Many applicants who give otherwise relevant information about themselves often omit essential facts. It is not unusual for the letter to contain no indication of the sex or age of the applicant.'

That statement, again, stresses the need to give the essential facts which have been listed above. It also stresses the need for neatness and legibility, and the absence of mistakes and corrections: in fact, stresses the need for drafting, checking, re-drafting and re-checking, before making a fair copy.

From Mr D came the following advice:

'Our general preference is for applications which are typed or legibly written, and which give concisely the relevant details regarding the applicant's age, education, training and experience. So many of the letters we receive tend to be very discursive, and give us anything but the information we really need.

'What influences us most in granting an interview is the experience or qualifications that the applicant appears to have, rather than the actual composition of his letter. The majority of those applying for jobs probably do give a considerable amount of thought to the composition of their letters, but in our experience the most satisfactory application is a short covering letter enclosing a typed sheet giving the full personal history of the applicant under appropriate headings.'

Two other large employers of labour kindly set down some useful guidance in 'potted' form for the benefit of applicants. One wrote:

'We feel strongly that any letter of application should
(1) be brief;
(2) contain certain basic facts about the candidate such as date of birth, nationality, whether single or married;
(3) mention any of the candidate's achievements, such as positions or responsibility attained, examinations passed (*with class of results*), &c.; and
(4) give the candidate's present position and salary (if this can be disclosed).

'We should add that the way in which any applicant phrases his letter does not normally affect whether or not he is called for an interview. It may, however, cut out the need for the filling in of an application form, or it may avoid his being turned down through his not having supplied enough information.'

The second employer also tabulated some of his requirements, and added much useful advice, as follows:

'The best application consists of a brief covering letter giving details of the position applied for, together with an attached sheet giving clear and concise information under the following headings:

(1) age;

(2) address—some indication of mobility is often interesting;

(3) training, giving dates;

(4) experience, giving dates;

(5) examinations passed—often information is given about examinations taken, but no indication is given whether they have been passed, and I normally interpret this as a failure;

(6) salary—this is not necessary for more junior positions, but it is very useful when applications are received from more senior men, so that one knows whether one's time is being wasted in giving consideration to the application.

'My own view,' he continues, 'is that in reading an application one wants to conjure up in one's imagination a true picture of the applicant, and with practice this can be done fairly accurately if information is given as above.

'I hope it is unnecessary to state that applications should be very clearly written, preferably typed, and that the English and spelling must be good. If one has to wade through a letter which is difficult to read, or where spelling and punctuation are suspect, it certainly does not give a good impression, and for many positions would rule the applicant out.

'I would also underline that no unnecessary frills are required and, in fact, are irksome. A statement of plain fact is what is required, and nothing more. Perhaps I should add that the type of applicant who sends a stencilled letter does not go down at all well, and almost automatically he will be rejected.'

A duplicated 'circular' letter should be used in the following circumstances only: an applicant may have a statement of his age, education, experience and so forth duplicated, for enclosing with a personally written letter; and duplicated letters are used by the officials of the Technical Register of the

Ministry of Employment and Productivity. They will circularise to a number of firms the particulars of an applicant, but they add a confidential appraisal of the man as they see him during an interview, which precedes all direct contact of the applicant with the company which may be interested in him.

The chief of the recruitment department of another very large company writes:

'There is no particular form of application letter that appeals to us more than any other, since we regard a letter as an expression of the applicant's personality.'

He follows with a useful list of 'do's' and 'don't's' for those who are planning letters of application. He writes:

'We look for

    (1) brevity consistent with adequate factual information;

    (2) clarity of thought and expression;

    (3) frankness and politeness;

    (4) correct grammatical construction, correct spelling and punctuation, and legible handwriting. If an applicant's signature is not clear, we expect him to print his or her name under it, and state sex if there is any possibility of confusion.

'We are put off by

    (1) all forms of flattery;

    (2) all expressions of servility;

    (3) glowing references which have no particular bearing on the application; and

    (4) stereotyped personal histories which are not clearly related to the advertised job specifications.'

When applying for some positions your prospective employer may ask for the names and addresses of two (or more) 'referees' who will testify to your good character, suitability for the post or previous training. They should be people who know you well, either through having been personal friends for some years, or through having educated, trained or employed you; or commanded you while you were in one of the Services, if they really did know you personally (and not just as 'Number Six in the rear rank').

Moreover, each of your referees should be a person of some standing in his profession or social circle; a magistrate, a clergyman, serving or retired officer, employer of labour, doctor, lawyer, official in national or local government service. Advertisers who ask for references usually 'take them up'— *ie* write to the referees whose names you give—and they need some indication that these referees are people on whom they may rely to give a truthful and informative reference.

If you have obtained written references or testimonials from previous employers, teachers or others who know you, enclose *copies* of them, but keep the originals. You may need to send copies to several prospective employers.

Finally, if you know that the position advertised demands physical strength which you do not possess, do not waste your time and the advertiser's by applying for it.

The following examples of letters of application for employment are intended only as models on which to shape your own letter. Fit your own circumstances to the most suitable of these models, sketch our your letter along the lines indicated, and then re-write it so that it expresses your own personality.

Shorthand Typist

Box No. . . . .
Daily ———
Fleet Street,
London, E.C.4.

Dear Sirs,
       With reference to your advertisement in today's *Daily* ———, I write to apply for the position of shorthand typist.

My age is 20, and I have been with my present employers (Messrs Blank, Dash & Company, Ltd, yarn merchants, St Mary Axe, E.C.3) for $3\frac{1}{2}$ years.

I was educated at Hendon High School, and gained GCE at O level in English and Geography when I was 16.

My speeds are: Shorthand 100 words per minute; Typing 60 words per minute. I am accustomed to taking dictation for long periods straight on to the typewriter, with considerable accuracy.

I believe that I have given my present employers full satisfaction, and they have given me increasingly responsible work to do. My reason for wishing to leave them is that I want to widen my experience. The terms stated in your advertisement are an advance on my present conditions of employment; and I feel sure that I could give you satisfactory and loyal service. My present employers have promised to give me a favourable reference.

                    Yours truly,
                      (Miss) ——— ———

Mechanical Engineer

The Personnel Manager,
X & Y Co., Ltd,
—— Street,
Bermondsey, London, S.E.1.

Dear Sir,
    I wish to apply for the vacancy for a fitter-mechanic advertised in today's *Daily* ——.

I am 23, single, and was educated at Sidcup Technical School, where I obtained GCE at O level in five subjects; and at the Imperial College of Science and Technology, London. I hold the City and Guilds of London Institute's certificate.

I have been employed for the last eighteen months by the Wolds Welding Company, Ltd, at their Birmingham works. I understand that my work gives full satisfaction, and my average weekly earnings have risen to £— with merit money but without overtime pay.

Now I wish to return to the London area, where my parents live. My mother is in poor health, and it is necessary for me to live at home to be able to help her and my father. As I wish also to extend my experience, and the terms stated in your advertisement include higher pay and interesting prospects of advancement, I hope that you will consider my application.

I could come for an interview at any time convenient to you next week, as my present employers know that I am writing to you, and have kindly promised to give me time off for that purpose. They have also given me a reference, a copy of which is enclosed.
    I am, Sir,
        Yours faithfully,
          R—— G. H——.

Publisher's Traveller

The Managing Director,
X & Y (Publishers) Ltd,
—— Street,
Strand, London, W.C.2.

Dear Sir,
    I am applying for the position of sales representative in the Midlands area which is advertised in today's *Daily* ——.

My present employment as a clerical assistant, grade two, in the Board of Trade is unestablished, and the prospects of advancement, and even of permanent employment, are virtually nil.

My age is 37, and I was formerly employed in the offices of Messrs Foreword and Preface, publishers of children's books, where I gained a sound general knowledge of book publishing.

I have some years' experience of driving several makes of cars and motorcycles, and although I do not at present own a car I hold a current and clean driving licence.

I am now anxious to return to the publishing business, in which I am keenly interested, and, although I have no experience of 'travelling' an area, I have confidence in my ability to learn quickly and to give satisfaction. I have kept up my subscription to the *Bookseller* since I was employed by Messrs Foreword and Preface, and I am well acquainted with present day trends in publishing, and especially with the books in your own recent lists.

I hope to hear from you that I may attend for an interview.

Yours faithfully,

P—— P——.

Junior Clerk

The Staffing Officer,
X Co., Ltd,
(address)

Dear Sir,

In reply to your advertisement in today's *Daily M——* I would like to apply for the post of junior clerk.

I am 17 and have recently left the Loamshire County High School for Girls, where I have been for the last five years.

Last summer I passed GCE at O level in Maths and German, and at A level in English and French. I was School Captain and Victrix Ludorum during my last year.

Since leaving school I have taken a private course in typing and shorthand, as well as attending evening classes in those subjects and in book-keeping and commercial practice.

I enclose a copy of a testimonial from my Headmistress, and I shall be glad to send you the names of two other people who know me well, and who would testify to my conduct and character.

I could come for an interview at any time convenient to you.

Yours respectfully,
(*signature*)

Chauffeur-handyman

The Lord Eastminster,
—— Grange,
————

My Lord,

I should like to be considered for the post of chauffeur-handyman advertised by you in today's *Daily M——*.

I am 38, single, and am at present employed as chauffeur by

Major Sir A—— B——. Besides my driving duties, I am responsible for the care, maintenance and minor repairs of the two cars, a Rolls Royce and a Humber Snipe.

As Sir A—— B—— is going away next month to live in Southern Portugal, and will not require me to accompany him, I shall be free to take up a new post on November 1 next.

I enclose copies of testimonials from Sir A——, with whom I have been for the last eight years, and from my previous employer, General Sir C—— D——, and hope that my application may receive your kind consideration.

> I am, my Lord,
> Yours respectfully,
> (*signature*)

Draper's Traveller

The Secretary,
X.Y.Z. Company, Ltd,
(address)

Dear Sir,

With reference to your advertisement in this week's *Draper's Record* for a Town traveller, I write to offer you my services.

I am 32, married, with two children. For the last six years I have been one of the Town travellers of A. B. & D. (Wholesale) Ltd, of Friday Hill, E.C.4. The company is going into voluntary liquidation, because of the death of the senior partner.

I am on excellent terms with the buyers in many of the larger London drapery stores, especially in the West End, and I feel sure that if I came to work for you I could increase my present yearly turnover of about £40,000.

I should hope to start with you at a salary of £— a year, with a — per cent commission on sales, and the usual expenses. I enclose copies of references from A. B. & D. and from my previous employers (—— & —— Ltd, of Hatch Street, E.C.) and I would be very pleased if you could give me an interview.

> Yours faithfully,
> (*signature*)

Technician

The —— Aeroplane Co., Ltd,
(address)

Dear Sirs,

In answer to your advertisement in today's *Daily M——* for draughtsmen I give the following brief particulars of my experience and qualifications:

1. Age 25. Married, two children.

2. *Education*: Loamshire Grammar School, and Loamshire Technical College. I passed GCE at O level in five subjects and A level in Maths, Physics and Engineering Drawing. Captain, School 1st XI cricket and association football.

3. *Previous employment:*

(i) Apprentice at —— 19—/19—.

(ii) Junior draughtsman with Messrs X & Y, at Z Aviation Works, 19—/19—.

(iii) I have been in the Drawing and Design Department of my present employers, —— & —— Ltd, since 19—.

4. I am applying for the advertised vacancy in your company because I wish to widen my experience of general aircraft design. I feel sure that I should do so in your employment.

5. I enclose copies of references from the three firms named above, and I have permission to come for an interview at any time convenient to yourselves.

Yours faithfully,
(*signature*).

Reporter

The Editor,
The —— *Gazette*,
(address)

Dear Sir,

I have heard from my friend Jonathan Marshall that he will be leaving your employment next month, and that therefore there will be a vacancy on your reporting staff. I submit the following summary of my experience, in applying for the post:

1. I am 26, single.

2. *Education*: City of Hull School, where I won form and school prizes for English Literature and Composition. I passed GCE at O level in six subjects and at A level in three. I was Captain of the XV, and Captain of Tennis; 6th Form, and a Prefect.

3. *Previous employment*: (*a*) Copy boy, then telephonist, on the —— *Express*, 19—/19—. (*b*) Junior reporter there from 19— to 19—, when I became a junior reporter on my present paper, the —— *Suburban News*. While here I have taken the training course under the National Council for the training of Journalists, which I completed satisfactorily last August.

4. My shorthand speed is now over 100 words per minute, I am a fast and accurate typist, and I have a thorough general experience of court reporting up to and including Assizes. I have also covered Sport, especially Rugger and Tennis.

I should be glad to come for an interview at any time which would suit you.

Yours faithfully,
(*signature*)

Personal Secretary

The Export Manager,
X & Y Ltd,
(address)

Dear Sir,
My friend Miss Eva Johnson has told me that she will be leaving her job as your personal secretary when she gets married in April. I know she has found the work interesting and has been very happy with you, and I am wondering if you would consider my application for the post.

Since I left school four years ago (I passed GCE at A level in three subjects) I have worked for —— & Co. Ltd, as junior clerk on general office duties, and relief telephonist. For the last two years I have been in the typing pool. I have taken a secretarial training college course in shorthand and typing (in which I have reached speeds of 100 and 60 words per minute) and in commercial practice.

I should very much like to join Messrs X & Y and gain experience of the work of a large firm. If I may come for an interview, perhaps you would let me know a day and time convenient to yourself.

Yours faithfully,
(*signature*)

ASKING FOR A RISE

It is impossible to indicate here to whom a letter asking for an increase in salary should be addressed as this will vary from firm to firm.

I

Dear X— X—,
I write to ask whether the Company can consider raising my salary. As you will know, I have been a member of the firm for eight years, two years have passed since I last had an increase, and a good deal of extra responsibility has fallen upon me this last year since Mr X's retirement.

My particular reason for making the request at this juncture is that my wife had a baby three weeks ago, our second child, and the need now arises to move from our flat to a small house, which we have found.

On my present salary, however, exercising every possible economy, I still do not feel we can take this step, and I should be most appreciative if the Company would consider my application.

Yours faithfully,
(*signature*)

2

John Brown, Esq.,
Managing Director,
X, Y & Co. Ltd,
(address)

Dear Sir,

I do not like talking to you about myself and my affairs, so I hope you will not mind if I first approach you in writing about an increase of salary.

The fact is that my salary is only £—— a year above the recognised minimum for the kind of work I am doing, and it has remained unchanged at that figure for twelve years.

When I joined the Firm in 19— my salary was £——. In 19— it was raised to £——, but since then I have received no further 'merit increase' although I have 12 years' more experience of the Company's work.

Moreover, I have frequently had sole charge of my department, often for spells of weeks when the manager and his deputy have been ill or on holiday. Yet I gather that I am receiving a lower salary than other employees of the Company who are in a similar position to mine, but are younger and have had shorter service with the firm.

I think I am entitled to point out that during my 17 years' total service with the Company I have been absent through illness for only six weeks in all. Four of those weeks of absence were caused by an injury received in a train accident.

On all these grounds I feel that I am justified in asking for an increase in my salary.

Yours faithfully,
(*signature*)

3

Private and Confidential

The Secretary,
The XYZ Co. Ltd,
(address)

Dear Sir,

As I hear that Mr —— will be leaving the Company's service at the end of next month, I write to apply for the post of departmental manager.

I have now been with the Company for 14 years, the last five of them in the —— Department under Mr ——, and I have often taken his place when he has been away on the Company's business, or on holiday.

I am well acquainted with the department's work, and I feel sure that I could carry it on efficiently, and perhaps increase its contribution to the Company's progress in a way that would satisfy the Board of Directors.

> I am, Sir,
> Yours faithfully,
> (*signature*)

4

Mrs John Smith,
(address)

Madam,

I am writing to make an application for an increase in my wages.

I have been in your service as cook now for the last 15 years, and I have been very happy to serve you and Mr Smith to the best of my ability. I believe that you have been satisfied with everything that I have done for you, and I do not think that you have ever had any cause for complaint about the meals and service.

However, my salary of £—— a year has not been increased for the last nine years, although the work has grown a lot, with more guests and dinner parties to cook for.

In these circumstances, Madam, and in view of the need I have to be able to save more for the time when I shall no longer be able to work for you, I think some increase in my wages is not an unreasonable thing to ask for, and I hope you will not think I am taking a liberty in writing to you about it.

> Your obedient servant,
> (*signature*)

5

Sir John Smith, KBE,
(address)

Dear Sir John,

I have now been your secretary for three years and during that time I believe that you have found my services useful and my work satisfactory. Indeed, you have been kind enough to tell me so on more than one occasion.

I hope, therefore, that you will consider favourably this application for an increase in my salary. I know you will bear in mind the many occasions when I have worked late; that I have always been punctual; and that much of the work that I have done for you has been of a confidential and often complicated nature.

I must add that I greatly appreciate your constant courtesy and kindness to me, and that I find the work both interesting and highly congenial.

Yours very truly,
(*signature*)

RESIGNING FROM A JOB

If an application for a rise is refused, you may well feel that it is time to move on.

Again, you may wish to seek other employment because you feel you have learned all you can in your present post and the prospects of advancement are small; maybe you are unhappy in your present employment, or think you can do better for yourself in a larger or a smaller firm. You may simply wish to move to another town to accept an offer made to you by another firm, or just want a change.

It is rude, ungrateful and altogether wrong—and it may, in some circumstances, be illegal—just to walk out of your employment and not go back. Your employer, whether you like him or not, is entitled to be treated courteously, and to be given a chance to find a replacement for you before you actually leave.

So you must 'give notice' before you leave your job. The length of notice depends on the terms agreed when you were engaged, or on the common custom of your kind of employment, or on what may be regarded as reasonable notice in the particular circumstances. Here are some sample letters showing how to give it:

I

John Jones, Esq.,
X, Y & Z,
(address)

Dear Sir,

I have given careful thought to what you said to me in the course of our interview. I fully appreciate that because the firm is not a large one, I cannot expect to receive the salary increase which I feel that my work and responsibilities deserve.

With reluctance, therefore, I have decided to take your advice, and to resign my employment as chief clerk. I shall try to find a position in a larger firm where I can hope that there will be more scope and better financial prospects.

I shall be glad if you will kindly give me a testimonial which would support the applications which I must make. I hope it will be convenient to you if I leave one month from today's date, i.e. on November 29th.

Yours truly,
(*signature*)

2

Messrs Smith & Smith,
(address)

Gentlemen,

I write to inform you that I have been appointed Head Buyer to Messrs X, Y & Co. and consequently I must give notice to terminate my employment with you on June 30.

I assure you that I have been most happy during the nine years of my employment with the Company, and I have met with nothing but kindness and consideration from all the Directors and Managers with whom I have been in contact, and with friendship from all my colleagues.

It is obvious that the training and experience which I have received during my service with the Company must have been largely responsible for the success of my application for my new position, and I am most grateful to all concerned.

I am, Gentlemen,
Yours truly,
(*signature*)

3

The Staff Manager,
Messrs X & Y.

Dear Mr ——,

I have recently been offered a post by Messrs —— which I believe gives me more opportunity for progress, and as they are prepared to pay me more than I am now earning, I have accepted their offer, which is however subject to a satisfactory reference. I hope and feel sure you will give this to me.

I would like to say at once that I shall in many ways be very sorry to leave your employment. Apart, however, from the considerations of better prospects in this new job and a higher salary, I think you will know that for some time I have not been too happy here due to a certain clash of personality. Nevertheless I shall always look back to my time at Messrs X & Y with gratitude for all that you and my colleagues have taught me.

My new firm would like me to join them at the beginning of June, so I hope it will be convenient if I leave in four weeks' time, on 31st May.

> Yours truly,
> (*signature*)

4

The Staff Manager,
Smythe & Smyth, Ltd,
(address)

Dear Sir,

A Birmingham firm has offered me a very good post as their Manchester representative, and I write therefore to give you formal notice to terminate my engagement with you one month from today's date.

> Yours faithfully,
> (*signature*)

The brevity and formality of that letter giving an employer notice of intention to leave might indicate that the writer was not happy in his work.

Here is a specimen of a less formal, but still brief letter of resignation:

5

D. Bell, Esq.,
General Manager,
XYZ Ltd,
(address)

Dear Mr Bell,

As my husband has been appointed to an excellent position with a firm in Aberdeen, we shall be moving our home there next month. I must, therefore, tender my resignation from the Company.

It has been a pleasure to work with you as your secretary during the last four years, and I wish to thank you for your kindness and consideration.

I hope it will be convenient if I leave two weeks today. Because of the move there will be a great deal to do.

> Yours sincerely,
> (*signature*)

GIVING A REFERENCE

There is one golden rule to bear in mind when giving references: if the prospective employer asks specific questions, and through experience you know of certain faults in the person for whom the reference is requested, answer only the questions asked. Employers can usually read between the lines. Of course if you know of any real reason why employment cannot be recommended you should say so. Naturally, if you think well of the person in question, you may add what praise you like, but try always to keep this relevant to the nature of the employment.

Here are examples of two references: no further comment should be needed.

1. In reply to your request I can confirm that —— has worked here for *x* months, and I have always found him/her sober, honest and hardworking.

2. I am delighted to give you this reference for ——. He/she has worked for me for *x* years and during that time I have always found him/her loyal, hardworking, intelligent and of complete integrity. He/she got on extremely well with the other employees of this firm and I personally shall be very sorry indeed to part with him/her. I recommend him/her to you with complete confidence and wish him/her the best of luck in his/her new job.

An open reference may be headed 'To whom it may concern', but the details would be the same as those shown above.

Here are further examples of references.

I

To Whom it may concern:

Mr J—— B—— has been manager of our export department for the last seven years, during which his energy, business acumen and initiative have been of great value to us. He has built up our export business considerably, and has a wide knowledge of the markets for our products and many useful contacts.

He is leaving us only because the business has been sold, and it gives us much pleasure to recommend him for any position where his ability and personal qualities can be given full scope.

(*signed*) Blank & Blank, Ltd.
(*in voluntary liquidation*)
James Smith-Blank.
Chairman and Managing Director.

2

Messrs X & Y,
Solicitors,
(address)

Gentlemen,

Miss Jones has left our employment as secretary to our senior partner because she is moving her home away from this town to an address within a short distance of your offices.

We have found her a first class secretary, and her work has been entirely satisfactory during the five years that she has been with us.

We are, Gentlemen,
Yours faithfully,
(*signature*)

3

Mrs M. James,
(address)

Dear Mrs James,

In reply to your inquiry, I am glad to be able to recommend M—— B—— as a housemaid. During her two years with me, she has been hard working and efficient, clean and tidy, polite and completely honest.

Her reason for wishing to leave me is that this house is somewhat isolated, and she is nervous when left alone, or when returning home from her evenings out.

I shall be sorry to part with her, and I wish her well in her future employment.

Yours very truly,
(*signature*)

4

The Staff Manager,
Messrs X Y & Z Ltd,
(address)

Dear Sir,

In reply to your request for information about John Smith, I am glad to be able to testify to his personal character. I have known him since he joined my Scout Troop seven years ago, and I have seen him grow up into a straightforward, honest and entirely trustworthy young man. He is quiet, well mannered and well spoken, yet always ready to tackle any task or any unexpected situation with which he is confronted.

He has worked hard to win several difficult badges, won the Queen's Scout award, and is now an assistant scoutmaster, helping to train other boys. His Scouting keenness, however, has never

come between him and his own work and education. He has
worked hard at evening classes with excellent results, which he
can tell you about himself. I cannot speak of his technical qualifications, but I have no hesitation in recommending him, from my
personal knowledge, for any position of trust, or one where
initiative and leadership would be required.

> Yours faithfully,
> (*signature*)
> Group Scout Leader,
> 1st Blanktown Group

5

To Whom it may concern:

This is to certify that John Smith has been a pupil at this
school for the last four years, during which his conduct has been
excellent and his school work very satisfactory. Had he been
able to stay at school longer he would undoubtedly have continued
to make good progress, and become a prefect. As it is, he passed
the GCE examination this summer at O level in English, Maths and
Mechanical Drawing.

He has taken a leading part in both Cricket and Rugby football
as a member of his House teams and the School second teams, and
has also been active in swimming and boxing. He won our junior
cross country race last year.

He is reliable, trustworthy and well mannered, and should do
well in any employment suited to his attainments. It is a great
pity that the loss of his father compels him to leave school now.

I shall be happy to do my best to supply any more information
that may be helpful.

> (*signed*) P—— R—— M.A.
> Headmaster.

6

Finally, here is an example of the kind of reference that
might be given in the case of someone whom the writer
regards without much favour.

To Whom it may concern:

Mr J—— B—— is leaving our employment because he seeks
a position with a higher salary than we are prepared to pay. He
has been with us for two years, and during that time we have always
found him trustworthy. We wish him success in his future career.

> (*signed*) Steel & Steel, Ltd.
> per pro James Jones
> Staff Manager.

It may be noted that if an employee has been dismissed and a request for a reference is received, the former employer is entitled to state the facts in a letter to the inquirer. But every statement in the letter must be made honestly and without malice; the letter should be headed 'Privileged and Confidential'; and the envelope marked 'Strictly Private and Personal'. But it is best to convey the information verbally in a private interview.

PRIVILEGE

The word 'privilege' used in the legal sense means that the speaker or writer cannot be successfully sued for libel, slander or defamation by anyone to whom he refers critically in public speech or written report; because of the place or circumstances in which he said or wrote his criticism. Members of Parliament, for instance, are privileged in their utterances inside the Houses of Parliament. So are judges, lawyers and witnesses in courts of law, and reporters and editors in their factual and immediate reports of proceedings in the courts.

An employer who gives a truthful and unmalicious reference about a departing employee is usually also covered by privilege, as is a manager who makes confidential reports to his employer about the firm's employees.

When an employer is asked by a departing employee for a reference he can refuse to give one. But if he gives one it must be written honestly and sincerely, without malice or prejudice, however much he may personally dislike the employee.

The decision whether to engage the applicant or not is for the new employer to make; but the former employer must give both his departing employee and the prospective new employer a fair chance to reach agreement, by giving a fair and unbiased opinion of the employee's capabilities, character and attainments.

It is not fair to recommend as honest and trustworthy a dishonest person to a prospective employer who may, in his turn, be robbed and cheated. But it is not fair to spoil the chances of a departing employee who has slipped but is trying to reform. A careful balance must be observed in respect of all letters of reference and recommendation.

MATTERS OF FORM

A DELIGHTFUL story was told of the Prince of Wales (Prince Charles) when he was a new boy, aged nine, at his preparatory school. As is the custom at such schools, every boy had to write a letter to his parents once a week; and on the first 'letter home day' of his first term he sat with the other boys of his form at their schoolroom desks.

The master in charge noticed that the prince's face bore a worried frown, and presently the boy laid down his pen and went up to the master's desk.

'I know my mother is Queen,' said Charles, 'but how do I put that on an envelope?'

How would you address an envelope to the Queen?

There are two correct ways of doing this, which may be called the formal and the personal styles. If you were a minister of the crown, or a lord mayor, or the holder of some official position, and you had to send an official communication—a report, a petition, a loyal address of congratulation—to the Queen, the address would be

To The Queen's Most Excellent Majesty.

But if your letter is of a more personal nature, such as an expression of thanks for an award, or if you have no official position of an administrative or representative kind, your envelope could fittingly be addressed

To Her Majesty the Queen.

As to the rest of the address on the envelope, the newspapers usually keep everyone fully informed of the Queen's whereabouts, so you can address your letter to her wherever she happens to be; viz., Buckingham Palace, London, SW1; Windsor Castle, Berkshire; Sandringham House, Norfolk; or Balmoral Castle, Aberdeenshire.

If your letter is a formal one you would begin (salutation):

May it please Your Majesty,

but if it is a personal one, begin it, simply,

> Madam.

In either case, the ending (subscription) should be:

> I have the honour to remain, Madam,
> Your Majesty's most humble and obedient servant,

followed by your signature and, below it, any rank or other special designation by which you are properly known.

But should you or I or Mrs Smith of Back Lane, Bermondsey, write to the Queen? Suppose that you have a grievance about your pension, or a claim to a reward, or a grandmother who will be a hundred years old next week: may you write to the Queen about it?

There is no law that forbids anyone writing to anyone else; so there is nothing to prevent anyone from writing to the Queen, and there is no punishment for doing so (provided that the letter itself is not unlawful).

But before you sit down and write 'May it please Your Majesty' just stop and think: what is likely to be the result? The Queen can act only on the advice of her Ministers in any kind of official matter. So write instead to the appropriate one, or to your MP. For a Royal message to a centenarian write four months in advance of the date, to The Assistant Private Secretary to the Queen, at Buckingham Palace.

Before setting out the correct forms of address, it will be helpful to survey briefly the various kinds of titles. Titles may be grouped into three classes: hereditary (which are passed on at death to the nearest lawful heir); non-hereditary (which die when the holder dies); and courtesy titles.

Hereditary titles (highest ranking first) are: duke, marquess, earl, viscount (pronounced *vy-count*) and baron; peeresses 'in their own right' (women who have inherited a title; only a few can be so inherited); and baronets, who are not 'lords' of any kind, but have the title 'Sir' placed before their forename. The first five named are all called peers. Baronets are not peers. Most peers but not all have the right to sit in the House of Lords, the upper house of our Parliament. The wives of peers are termed peeresses, but not 'in their own right'. Peeresses 'in their own right', including Life Peeresses but *not* peeresses by marriage, are entitled to sit in the House of Lords. Peers of Ireland who have no other British

United Kingdom title are *not* so entitled, but may be elected MPs.

Non-hereditary titles are: Law Lords—certain distinguished judges on whom the rank of baron is conferred, but for life only; Life Peers and Life Peeresses, with the rank for life of baron or baroness; the Scottish Lords of Session (judges) and the chairman of the Scottish Land Court, all of whom have 'bench titles' and are styled 'Lord ——' but are not (as are English law lords, and life peers and peeresses) members of the House of Lords; and Knights, who have the title 'Sir' placed before their forenames (like baronets).

Courtesy titles are the titles used by children, and in some cases grandchildren, of peers. Holders of courtesy titles are not themselves peers, nor members of the House of Lords. Almost all dukes, marquesses and earls have additional titles of lower degree, and the eldest son usually uses the highest of these lesser titles. A duke may have several lesser titles, marquess of This, earl of That and The Other, and viscount and baron of several more places too. The eldest son will use the highest (usually) of these, and will be styled by courtesy 'Marquess of Flint' (or whatever the title may be). And *his* eldest son will be addressed by one of the other titles of his grandfather the duke, but of a lower grade than his father's.

The younger sons of dukes and marquesses, and the daughters of dukes, marquesses and earls, are styled by courtesy 'Lord' or 'Lady' before their forename and family surname. The younger sons of earls, and all children of viscounts and barons, are styled 'The Hon.' before their forename and family surname. 'The Hon.' is a contraction of 'The Honourable' and the full form is used in speaking of them. But they are never spoken *to* as 'The Honourable' (or 'The Hon.') but as Mr, Mrs or Miss. The style may be used on an envelope, in the form 'The Hon.' or 'The Honble' but few would worry if it were omitted.

A title peculiar to Scotland is 'The Master of——'. This is borne by the eldest son, or next heir of all peers of Scotland, although it is usually not used if he has a courtesy title, one of his father's lesser titles. The wife of a 'Master', if he is the son of a peer, is 'The Hon. Mrs' followed by her husband's surname.

Another peculiarity of the Scottish peerage styles is that a

peer of the rank of baron is not styled 'Baron Blank', because
the term 'barony' has a special legal meaning in Scotland connected with land holding. He is always 'Lord Blank', even in
official documents. Elsewhere, a baron of the English,
Irish or United Kingdom peerages is only called 'Baron Blank'
in official documents, or in general terms (eg, 'Death of a
Baron'). Otherwise, he is always addressed in speech and
writing as 'Lord Blank'.

There are many other complications, special rules and
usages, exceptions and variations, in titles of honour, but
these are dealt with in the standard reference books on the
peerage and in specialised books about titles (see p. 151).

Several people bear designations which include the word
'Lord' who may or may not be peers; and there are others who
are properly addressed as 'My Lord' who are not peers at
all, although some of them are members of the House of
Lords, eg, some judges and bishops.

Another matter which must be touched on briefly here,
however, is the placing of initial letters after people's names
which indicate honours, decorations, university degrees,
membership of learned, scientific or professional societies and
so forth. A few broad groupings are possible: first come
honours and decorations conferred by the Crown, including
certain medals; secondly, those representing certain official or
legal distinctions; and then those of university degrees,
professional diplomas, and membership of professional and
similar bodies.

There are nine great Orders of Chivalry in Britain, consisting of one, three or five grades; and several other high
ranking honours, and many lesser decorations, which may
also be conferred on the Queen's subjects. Information about
these can be found in the reference books; the various sets of
initials which represent these honours, and their order of
precedence, is as follows:

 VC, GC, KG, PC, KT, KP, GCB, OM, GCSI, GCMG,
GCIE, VA, CI, GCVO, GBE, CH, KCB, KCSI, KCMG,
KCIE, KCVO, KBE, CB, CSI, CMG, CIE, CVO, CBE,
DSO, MVO (4th class), OBE, ISO, MVO (5th class), MBE,
RRC, DSC, MC, DFC, AFC, ARRC, AM, DCM, CGM, GM,
QPM, QFSM, DSM, MM, DFM, AFM, BEM, SGM, VD,
TD, ED, RD, VRD.

The following points should be noted:

1. The initials are always in CAPITAL letters. There is no need to put a full stop after each letter.

2. If a person holds three or more decorations or distinctions, use only the highest ranking one, followed by '&c'. If he has no more than two, write both: or one, if he has but one. In the case of official or other civilian initials of distinction, at least two may be written.

3. The precedence of civilian distinctions is not easy to define, but one general rule is that the more lasting the honour, the nearer its initials are placed to the holder's name. Thus, a man may be a Justice of the Peace for forty years, but a Member of Parliament for only two or three; so the order of placing the letters is 'J. Smith, Esq., JP, MP'. Similarly, a barrister who has 'taken silk' (*ie*, become a Queen's Counsel) and has also been elected to Parliament would be 'J. Smith, Esq., QC, MP', because he never ceases to be entitled to write QC after his name for the rest of his life (unless he is made a High Court Judge) but he may lose his seat at the next Parliamentary election.

The following points should also be noted:

4. Service rank comes first, before any title: *eg*, Major The Earl of Bournemouth; Commander The Lord Poplar, RN.

5. A baronet has 'Sir' before his names and the abbreviation 'Bt' after his surname, before the initials of any honours he may possess. (Note: the correct abbreviation is 'Bt' and *not* 'Bart', and it is wrong to refer to a baronet as 'a Bart'.)

The initials that indicate official positions are not many in number. The chief ones are QC, JP, MP, CC, DL. The initials CC for County Councillor are sometimes preceded by a letter indicating the name of the county: *eg*, GLC for a member of the Greater London Council, KCC for Kent, and so on. But these are used only within the county of which the person is a county councillor; otherwise there would be confusion between councillors of Lancashire, Leicestershire and Lincolnshire-Lindsey, for example.

These distinctions are, in fact, not used socially (*ie*, on personal letters), except QC and MP. The others are generally

confined to official lists, reports in local newspapers, dinner
guest lists, and similar occasions. The rule of 'permanent
before temporary' applies. All these 'official' initials follow
any honours conferred by the Crown, such as KBE or DSO
or MC or MVO.

It will be noted that DL, which stands for Deputy Lieutenant (of a county), is included, but not LL, which might be
thought to be appropriately placed after the name of the Lord
Lieutenant of a county. In fact LL is never used; because
officially there is no such person as a Lord Lieutenant. He is
'Her Majesty's Lieutenant for the County of ——' and
occasionally one sees the initials HML appended to the name
of a Lord Lieutenant; but there is no official recognition of this
practice. The initials DL are not among the 'Crown appointed' honours, because each Deputy Lieutenant is appointed by the Lieutenant of the county to be his deputy, not
by the Crown. Only the Lieutenant is appointed by the
Crown.

Last of all come university degrees, college diplomas,
honorary fellowships of learned societies, and initials indicating membership of various professional organisations,
some of which are earned by passing examinations and some
acquired by the payment of fees or subscriptions. There is
an enormous number of these distinctions, and no clear rules
are laid down about their order of precedence, or their use in
correspondence. The only general rule is that they should be
used when writing or referring to someone in his capacity
as a member of the profession or other body concerned, but
not in ordinary social correspondence. The exception to this
rule is the university degree of doctor, which may always be
used in speech and correspondence. Some would add the
(comparatively rare) distinction denoted by the initials FRS
(Fellow of the Royal Society) in correspondence (not in speech).

Your family doctor may not be a 'doctor' at all, in the
technical sense; that is to say, he may not have a university
degree (a 'doctorate') as a Doctor of Medicine (MD) which
alone, in the medical profession and the world of science,
entitles him to be styled 'Doctor' officially. He may have
university degrees as a bachelor of medicine and a bachelor of
surgery; or he may have the diplomas (not degrees) of the
colleges of physicians and surgeons, or the Society of Apothe-
caries, all of which entitle him to be registered and to practise

as a doctor. Whatever his qualifications, he (or she) will not object to being addressed in speech or correspondence as 'Doctor' with the exception of the specialist in surgery. He is always Mr.

Many people who possess doctorates, and are entitled to be styled 'Doctor', are not medical practitioners. There are doctorates in various branches of Science (DSc.) and in Laws, Literature, Philosophy, and so on. Most Anglican bishops and many other clerics are Doctors of Divinity.

If you are writing to your medical practitioner, therefore, and you wish to address the envelope correctly, you should find out what his qualifications are. They are usually stated on his brass plate, and his notepaper. If he is an MD you may address the envelope either to

Dr John Smith

or to   John Smith, Esq., MD.

and although he may have several other qualifications it is not necessary to put any more. If he has served in the Armed Forces in wartime and been decorated, you would write that as well, thus:

Dr John Smith, MC

or   John Smith, Esq., MC, MD.

But if you find on inquiry in the reference books that he does not possess a doctorate, you may address the envelope to either 'Doctor' (by courtesy) or 'Mr' or as in the second example above (name followed by 'Esq.') and with a pair of his qualifications; *eg,*

John Smith, Esq., MB, BCh.
or   John Smith, Esq., MRCS, LRCP
or   John Smith, Esq., DSC, MB, BS.

In the case of a woman doctor, you must ascertain whether she is Mrs or Miss. It is usually easier to address her as

Dr Mary Brown, MB, BS

or whatever her medical qualifications may be. This avoids all risk of addressing a married woman doctor who may be widowed, or divorced, as 'Miss', or of conferring married status on an unmarried woman.

No one should be addressed as 'Professor' unless he occupies a professorial chair in a university. Assistant professors, lecturers and demonstrators in universities and colleges do not rate as Professor for purposes of address in speech or correspondence. A professor who has a doctor's degree is not, in Great Britain, addressed as 'Professor Doctor Smith', although that is the practice followed in some countries. Laymen, such as swimming teachers, magical entertainers and unqualified 'healers' who style themselves 'Professor' or 'Doctor' should *not* be so addressed.

Honorary doctorates and similar distinctions conferred on Royal and other personages who are distinguished in other walks of life than the academic do not use them, and the initials indicating such honours should not be appended to their names on envelopes. For instance, Queen Elizabeth the Queen Mother has accepted the honorary degree of DCL and DLitt., but those initials would not be placed after her name on an envelope.

As to other fellowships and memberships, the initials should be used only in connection with the activities which they indicate. If you are writing to an architect about architectural work, add the initials showing fellowship of his professional body to his name—FRIBA—provided that you know he is entitled to use them. If you are writing to the secretary of a company who, you know, is entitled to the letters ACIS or FCIS, use them. But these are not used in social letters.

An exception may be made for FRS, and for the letters indicating proficiency in the Arts: RA and ARA, RSA and ARSA, and PRA and PRSA. These may be used on social and official correspondence if desired. But non-academic 'fellowships' such as those of the Royal Geographical and Historical Societies, the Zoological Society and so forth, should not be used in correspondence, because they are granted without any proof of special academic attainment or active achievement.

Finally, it should be repeated that there is no law or regulation about all this. No one can be fined or imprisoned for writing

John Smith Esq., FRHS,

on the envelope containing an invitation to a garden party. But anyone who invites people to accord him the initials of honours, decorations, titles or official distinctions to which he is not entitled, with intent to defraud, may lay himself open to prosecution.

Where there are established forms of addressing certain people, it is rude and churlish to ignore them, or to use the wrong form. Although the recognised authorities on these matters are not always unanimous about the correct form, the following guide to good manners in addressing titled and official persons may be helpful. To save time and space, names are usually represented by letters of the alphabet. The actual names and addresses may be found in reference books at a public library.

The usual manner of subscribing a letter to titled, &c., people is:

> I have the honour to be,
>> My Lord (*or* Sir, *or* Your Grace)
> Your Lordship's (&c.) obedient servant,

when the letter is of an official nature, or is written to someone who is not personally known to you. The social manner, as in a letter on an informal subject, or one sent to a personal acquaintance or friend, is:

> Yours very sincerely,

or some similar form.

The general system followed in the following guide is to give first the form of address as it should appear on the envelope, followed where necessary by the form of salutation; and, in some cases, the special style of subscription where this differs materially from the usual style shown above. The forms of address for letters to wives of titled people are to be found under the husband's title; *eg*, for the way to address a countess, see under 'Earl'. Verbal forms of address are not given; this book is concerned only with letter writing. The guide includes official, legal and religious dignitaries as well as titled people, and begins with:

ABBOT   The Right Revd The Abbot of
                         A——

  Begin: My Lord Abbot, *or* Right Revd
                         Father

End: I beg to remain, my Lord Abbot
                              (*or* Rt Rvd Father)
                                 Your devoted and obedient
                                 servant

Note : Those are the forms which a Roman Catholic should use, but the title of 'Abbot' or 'Lord Abbot' is not officially recognised in the United Kingdom, and is not used by non-Catholics, who would address the envelope to

                              The Right Revd B—— C——
                              (using his name)

and begin the letter: Right Reverend Sir.

ALDERMAN   Mr Alderman A—— B——

Begin: Dear Sir *or* Dear Mr Alderman
                              B——

AMBASSADOR   His Excellency Lord A—— (*or*
                              Sir B—— C——)

Begin: My Lord or Sir (whichever is
                              the case)

End: I have the honour to be,
                              My Lord (*or* Sir),
                              Your Excellency's obedient
                              servant

Notes : Address an ambassador's wife according to her own rank as the wife of a peer, baronet, knight, peer's daughter, &c. She is not entitled to be addressed as 'Her Excellency' although this courtesy is sometimes accorded.

ARCHBISHOP   His Grace The Lord
(Anglican)   Archbishop ——

Begin: My Lord Archbishop,
  or   Your Grace

End: I have the honour to remain,
                              My Lord Archbishop,
                              Your Grace's devoted and
                              obedient servant

A retired archbishop is addressed as

> The Most Revd Archbishop E——

or, if he has received a peerage,

> The Most Revd Lord F——.

An archbishop's wife is only Mrs D—— E——, whether her husband is active or retired (Lady F—— if he has been created a peer).

A Roman Catholic archbishop is addressed by a Catholic as

> His Grace the Archbishop of G——

Begin: as for Anglican

End: as for Anglican except last line,

which should be

> Your Grace's devoted and obedient child.

A non-Catholic might suitably end as follows:

> I have the honour to be,
> Your faithful servant

ARCHDEACON   The Venerable J—— K——

or   The Venerable The Archdeacon of——

Begin: Venerable Sir

or   Dear Mr Archdeacon

End: I have the honour to remain, Venerable Sir,
> Your obedient servant

Notes: A retired archdeacon does not (or should not) continue to use or receive these styles. As an ordinary clergyman he reverts to 'The Revd J—— K——'. But if, on retirement, he has the honorary style of archdeacon conferred on him, he is still 'Venerable'.

BARON	The Right Hon. The Lord M——
(informally)	The Lord M——
Begin (formally):	My Lord
(informally)	Dear Lord M——
End:	I have the honour to remain, Your Lordship's obedient servant

BARONESS (by inheritance or Life Peeress)	The Rt Hon. Baroness L——
or	The Rt Hon. Lady L——
(by marriage)	The Baroness L——
or	The Lady L——
Begin:	Madam (*not* 'My Lady')
End:	I have the honour to be Your most obedient servant

Notes: A baron's son is addressed as 'The Hon. John M——' and the letter begins 'Sir'. A baron's unmarried daughter is 'The Hon. Mary M——'. If married to an untitled person, she is 'The Hon. Mrs N——'. If married to a knight or a baronet, she is 'The Hon. Lady N——'. If married to anyone with a higher title than that of baronet, she has the appropriate style without 'the Hon.'. The formal style of salutation in all cases is 'Madam'.

BARONET	Sir Charles James, Bt
Begin:	Dear Sir or Dear Sir Charles (the latter is informal)

His wife is Lady James (no forename).

His widow would continue to be 'Lady James' unless the new baronet is married, or marries, when the widow would be 'Mary, Lady James' (but *not* 'Lady Mary James').

BISHOP (All bishops of the Anglican or other Protestant Churches, with the exception of assistant bishops.):

The Right Revd The Lord
Bishop of——

Begin: My Lord Bishop

End: Your Lordship's most obedient
servant

Anglican bishops have a particular way of signing their
names; for information about this, and a list of their signatures, see page 147.

Assistant bishops should be addressed

The Right Revd Bishop J. N——

Retired bishops should be addressed

The Right Revd John N——

Sometimes peers are also clergymen, or a clergyman may
inherit a peerage, and he is then styled 'The Revd The Lord
B——' and *not* 'The Lord Revd B——'. If he is given the
full style for a baron, he is 'The Revd The Right Hon. The
Lord B——'. A retired bishop who is also a privy councillor
is styled 'The Rt Hon. and Rt Rev. P—— B——'.

Bishops of the Episcopal Church in Scotland, and of the
Roman Catholic Church there (and in England and Wales)
would be addressed as 'The Rt Rev. S—— T——, Bishop
of Midlothian' (or elsewhere), and *not* as 'The Rt Rev. The
Lord Bishop of ——', in official correspondence, or by non-
members of their Church.

A Roman Catholic should address a letter to a Roman
Catholic bishop in England

The Right Revd A—— B——,
Bishop of ——

or   His Lordship the Bishop of ——.

He would salute him as 'My Lord' or 'My Lord Bishop' and
end:

I have the honour to remain,
Your Lordship's obedient
child.

In Ireland, every bishop is addressed (officially, in the Republic of Ireland, and by all Roman Catholics) as

The Most Revd The Bishop of ——.

All Roman Catholic bishops (and archbishops) of titular sees (ancient Christian sees which are no longer actually occupied or administered) are addressed as 'The Most Revd'.

Anglican bishops whose spheres of activity lie in other countries must be accurately addressed, if offence is not to be given to non-Anglicans. Those who work outside the British Commonwealth are therefore styled as follows:

The Right Revd The Lord Bishop *in* (not *of*) Argentina, &c.; Egypt; Iran; Jerusalem; Korea; Madagascar; Sudan. The Bishop of Fulham, who is a suffragan of the Bishop of London, is also 'Bishop *for* (not *in*) North and Central Europe', visiting Anglican churches in many countries.

The wife of a bishop is 'Mrs John Smith' on envelopes (unless her husband has a secular title which he has inherited). She is not addressed as 'My Lady' even if her husband has been granted an honorary knighthood.

Lastly on this subject, it is always wise to check a name or title in a reference book. Your public library probably has a copy of *Crockford's Clerical Directory* which is the guide to all dignitaries, clergy, dioceses and parishes of the Church of England; and the Year Book or *Who's Who* which is issued by other Churches.

CANON	The Revd Canon C—— D——
Begin:	Reverend Sir
or	Dear Canon D——

In the Roman Catholic Church a canon is addressed:

	The Very Revd Canon C—— D——
Begin:	Very Reverend Sir
CARDINAL	His Eminence Cardinal E—— (surname only)

or, if an Archbishop	His Eminence the Cardinal Archbishop of W——
Begin:	My Lord, *or* My Lord Cardinal
End:	I have the honour to remain, My Lord, Your Eminence's devoted and obedient child

A non-Catholic could fittingly use the following forms:

	His Eminence Cardinal E—— (but not the alternative)
Begin:	My Lord Cardinal
End:	I have the honour to remain, Your Eminence's obedient servant

CHAIRMAN OF GLC	The Right Hon. The Chairman of the Greater London Council

Notes: He is the only chairman of a county council, or any other municipal council, who is entitled to be styled 'The Right Honourable' except those councils which are presided over by a Lord Mayor or a Lord Provost to whom this honour has been specifically granted. (See Lord Mayor, Lord Provost, Privy Councillor.)

CHANCELLOR (Church)	The Worshipful Chancellor F——
Begin:	Sir or Dear Sir

Address a University Chancellor according to his (or her) rank; Chancellor of the Exchequer, and of the Duchy of Lancaster, as for a Privy Councillor; Chancellor of County Palatine of Durham as 'His Honour' followed by name; Lord Chancellor, see under that heading.

CHIEF RABBI	The Very Revd The Chief Rabbi
Begin:	Very Revd and dear Sir
CLERGY	The Revd John Smith

This is the correct style of address for vicars, rectors, curates and all ordained clergy of the Church of England, curates and all ordained clergy of the Church of England, ministers of the Church of Scotland and ministers and pastors of other Protestant Churches. (See also 'PRIEST' and 'RABBI'.) It is entirely wrong to write 'The Revd Smith' and even worse to write 'Rev. Smith'. (For peers who are clergymen, see page 75.)

CONSUL   John K——, Esq.,
                            HBM Consul at —— (or Consul-
                                General)

  Begin: Sir,

COUNTESS See 'Earl'

DAME   Dame Joan Brown, GBE (or
                                DBE)

  Begin: Madam,
    or (informally)   Dear Dame Joan

Notes: This ancient title was revived for women when the two grades which confer the dignity of knighthood on a man, in each of three of the Orders of Chivalry, were opened to women, to whom they may be given for useful services to Queen or nation. The three Orders are the Royal Victorian Order and the Order of the British Empire, each of which has five classes, and the Order of St Michael and St George, which has three classes. The two highest classes in each Order are styled, for men, Knight Grand Cross, and Knight Commander; and these honours, when conferred on a woman, give her the title of Dame (Dame Grand Cross, Dame Commander), corresponding to the men's title of Knight or prefix Sir. As with knights, the forename must always be used after 'Dame'. We do not address a knight as 'Sir Smith' but as 'Sir John Smith, KBE' (or whatever it may be). So a woman who has received a similar honour must be 'Dame Jane Smith, DBE' and so on, and addressed as 'Dame Jane' (*not* 'Dame Smith').

The title 'Dame' is not used if she has a higher title, but the initials are always placed after her name or title.

DEAN   The Very Revd The Dean of
                                A——

  Begin: Very Reverend Sir
    or (informally)   Dear Mr Dean

Note: A dean who is a former bishop is addressed

> The Right Revd The Dean of
> A——

A retired dean should not be styled 'Very Revd' unless the title of 'Dean Emeritus' has been conferred on him, when he may be addressed

> The Very Revd J—— K——

Otherwise, a retired dean (who is not also a retired bishop) reverts to his 'substantive rank' as a clergyman, and is addressed

> The Revd J—— K——

DOWAGER	Her Grace The Dowager Duchess of Rye
Begin: *or*	Madam Dear Duchess of Rye (*informal*)
End:	Madam, Your Grace's most obedient Servant Yours sincerely (*informal*)

A dowager peeress, except in Scotland, is the earliest surviving widow of a previous holder of the title, no matter what relation she is to the present holder. She may be his mother, grandmother, aunt, &c. If her late husband's successor dies, leaving a widow, the dowager continues to be the dowager peeress, and the new widow is known by her forename prefixed to the title;

eg,

> Her Grace Mary, Duchess of
> Rye.

although nowadays the senior of two Dowager Duchesses also often prefers to use the form 'Mary, Duchess of Rye'.

In Scotland, only the mother or the grandmother of the holder of the title is styled Dowager, the mother assuming it on the death of the grandmother.

DUKE	His Grace The Duke of Rye
Begin:	My Lord Duke

End:	I remain
	    Your Grace's most obedient
	    servant

The forms of address for a duke's wife, widow and widowed mother are shown in the examples under 'Dowager' (above) although the styles there set out apply to all ranks of peers, of which Duke is the highest.

Begin:	Madam (*not* 'My Lady Duchess'!)
End:	as for a Duke

EARL	The Right Hon. The Earl of Kew
Begin:	My Lord. *Informally*, Dear Lord Kew
End:	I remain, Your Lordship's most obedient servant

The wife of an earl, the third grade of the peerage, is styled Countess, and formally addressed as

	The Right Hon. The Countess of Kew
Begin:	Madam
End:	as for an Earl (but 'Ladyship's')

ENVOY	J. Smith, Esq., HBM Envoy-Extraordinary
Begin:	Sir *or* Dear Sir

An 'Envoy-Extraordinary and Minister Plenipotentiary' is a diplomatic representative abroad, in charge of a Legation, which ranks below an Embassy in importance.

ESQUIRE This form of address is dealt with on page 32.

FOREIGN TITLES The titles used by foreigners (*ie* titles not conferred by a British Sovereign) are many and various, and the usages in other countries differ from British, as do the words by which titles and forms of address are expressed. Failing exact knowledge of the correct style appropriate to a foreign titled person, it is permissible to use the English terms for a British titled person of equivalent rank.

In some countries, the title 'Prince' has been bestowed on non-royal subjects (*eg*, Prince Bismarck) and they, their wives and their descendants would be correctly styled 'His (or Her) Highness'—*not* 'Royal Highness'.

GOVERNOR   His Excellency Sir P—— R——,
                 Governor of British Orkland

or   His Excellency John Smith, Esq.,
                 Governor and Commander-in-Chief,
                 The British Orkland Isles

Similarly for a Governor General or Lieutenant Governor. The style of a Lt-Gov. of a Canadian Province is 'His Honour'.

Begin: My Lord *or* Sir

The style 'Excellency' is officially accorded to the wife of a Governor General only. Governors' wives are not 'Excellencies'.

Begin: Madam

HIGH COMMISSIONER   His Excellency [1]
                 the High Commissioner for ——

Begin: Sir

or (informally)   Dear High Commissioner

HONOURABLE   The Honble John Doe

or   The Hon. Mary Roe

Notes: The style or title of 'The Honourable' is borne by the sons (except the eldest, who has a courtesy title) of all earls; by the sons and daughters of all viscounts and barons; and by the wives of the sons—but *not* by the husbands of the daughters, unless the husbands are entitled to it of their own right.

It is also borne by all Justices of the High Court (but *not* by Lord Justices) and, in Scotland, by all judges of the Court of Session. In the British Dominions, and also in the United States of America, this title is borne by the holders of many offices: judges, senators, provincial administrators, cabinet ministers, &c.

The following points should be noted:

1. Although the title is 'The Honourable' it is never written in full, always contracted. It is often written 'The Hon.' but looks better as 'The Honble'.

2. It is used *only* on envelopes of letters, and in that part of a letter called the direction (see page 18).

3. It is *never* used on visiting cards, or in public speech, in private conversation or in announcing a guest. It should not be used in listing bridesmaids, wedding guests, debutantes at parties, or in any place other than on an envelope.

Begin:	Sir, or dear Sir (or Madam)
End:	I have the honour to be, Sir, Your obedient servant

JUDGE: HIGH COURT   The Hon. Mr Justice A——

Begin: My Lord

Although addressed in writing as 'Mr Justice' they are always addressed and referred to in court as My Lord or Your (or His) Lordship. They are always knighted on appointment, but the style 'Sir John S——' is used only socially (*not* in Court) or after retirement. The prefix 'The Hon.' is not used socially, or after retirement.

COUNTY
COURT   His Honour Judge B——
Begin: Sir, or Dear Sir
              (*socially*, Dear Judge B——)

He is addressed and referred to as His Honour and Your Honour (*not* 'Judge') on the Bench. The title 'His Honour' is

retained after retirement, and a retired county court judge is
addressed

His Honour John B——

COURT OF
SESSION   The Honble Lord C——

Begin: My Lord

He is always, in or out of court, addressed and referred to as
My Lord and His Lordship, although these judges are not
peers. The title of Lord and the prefix 'The Hon.' are retained after retirement. His wife (or un-remarried widow) is
styled 'Lady'. Letters to her are addressed:

The Lady C——

JUSTICE OF THE
PEACE   John Smith, Esq., JP.

or   Mrs J. Smith, JP.

Although addressed verbally as 'Your Worship' when
sitting 'on the bench' in his court, this term is not used otherwise. In a letter, begin:

Dear Sir

or   Madam

KNIGHT   Sir John Jones

Begin: Sir

or   Dear Sir John

The above applies to 'knights bachelor' which is the lowest
order of knighthood. He is distinguished from an ordinary
'Mr' or 'Esq.' only by the prefixed title 'Sir'. It is *not* correct
to write 'kt' or 'knt' or KB after his name.

Ranking above a knight bachelor is a knight of any of the
Orders of Chivalry, of which there are nine in Great Britain
(though three of them are no longer awarded). Details of
these may be found in reference books. In addressing a letter
to a knight of one of these Orders, it is important to put the
right initials after his name, thus:

Sir John Jones, KCVO

or   Sir Peter Smith, GCB

LADY	(1) Lady Green
	(2) Jane, Lady Green
	(3) The Lady Green
	- (4) The Lady Jane Green
	(5) The Lady John Green
	(6) The Hon. Lady Green
Begin, in all cases:	Madam (formally)
or (informally)	(1), (2), (3) and (6)
	Dear Lady Green
	(4) Dear Lady Jane
	(5) Dear Lady John
End:	Yours faithfully
or	Your sincerely (*informal*)

These are six possible ways of correctly using the title 'Lady' on an envelope; the style depends on her rank.

In (1) she may be the wife of a knight, or of a baronet; or she may be the widow of either a knight, or of a baronet, whose successor has not married.

In (2) she may be the widow of a knight or a baronet whose successor has married; his wife is 'Lady Green' so the dowager, to distinguish her from the wife, is either 'The Dowager Lady Green' or, more usually, as shown.

The example (3) shows that she is a life peeress, or a peeress in her own right, or the wife of a baron, Lord Green. On an envelope the word 'The' indicates this.

(4) shows that she is the daughter of a duke, marquess or earl. She may be unmarried, Green being her family surname; or she may be married to a man whose surname is Green.

(5) shows that she is married to a younger son of a duke or a marquess (her husband's family surname being Green).

(6) shows that she or her husband is an 'Honble', and her husband a knight or baronet.

Style (2) may be used for the ex-wife, of a knight or baronet, whose former husband has re-married. She does not retain title if she re-marries and her husband is a commoner.

LORD ADVOCATE	The Right Honble The Lord Advocate
Begin:	Sir
or	Dear Lord Advocate

| LORD CHIEF JUSTICE | The Right Honble The Lord Chief Justice of England |
| Begin: | My Lord |

LORD JUSTICE-GENERAL	The Right Honble The Lord Justice-General of Scotland
Begin:	Dear Lord Justice-General
or	My Lord

He is the head of the High Court of Justiciary, the supreme criminal court of Scotland; and as Lord President of the Court of Session he is also head of the civil judiciary.

LORD JUSTICE OF APPEAL	The Right Honble Lord Justice A——
Begin:	My Lord
or	Sir

A Lord Justice of Appeal is always a knight and a privy councillor (hence the style of 'Right Honble') but is not a peer or 'lord' unless he has inherited a peerage.

LORD LIEUTENANT He is addressed by his title or rank and name, with the addition of

| | HM Lieutenant of C—— |
| Begin: | Sir *or* Dear Sir (*or* according to title) |

LORD MAYOR The Lord Mayors of London, York, Bristol, Belfast, Cardiff, Dublin, and the six State capitals of Australia (Adelaide, Brisbane, Hobart, Melbourne, Perth and Sydney) are entitled to the prefix 'Right Honourable' before the title of their office, while they hold the office. Address:

> The Right Honble The Lord Mayor of L——

All other Lord Mayors are addressed

> The Right Worshipful The Lord Mayor of N——

| Begin: | My Lord |
| (informally) | Dear Lord Mayor |

Note: the wife of a lord mayor is addressed

> The Lady Mayoress of M——

She is not entitled to the prefix 'Right Honble' but may be styled 'My Lady' when beginning a letter to her, or in speech.

LORD OF APPEAL   (addressed as for BARON)

LORD OF SESSION   (see page 83 under Court of Session)

LORD PRESIDENT (of the Court of Session)

> The Right Honble The Lord President of the Court of Session
> (of the Privy Council—according to his rank)

LORD PRIVY SEAL (addressed according to his rank)

LORD PROVOST (the civic head of certain cities in Scotland: he corresponds to the Lord Mayor of certain cities in England and elsewhere)

The Lord Provost of Edinburgh is addressed:

> The Right Honble The Lord Provost of Edinburgh

The Lord Provost of Glasgow is addressed:

> The Right Honble The Lord Provost of Glasgow

Other Lord Provosts (of Aberdeen, Dundee, Elgin and Perth) are addressed:

> The Lord Provost of A——

Begin: Dear Lord Provost

The wife of a lord provost has no title. She is 'Mrs A—— B——' and should *not* be styled 'Lady Provost'.

MARQUESS   Most Honble The Marquess of C——

Begin: (*officially*)   My Lord Marquess. *Informally*

(*informally*)   Dear Lord C——

End:	I have the honour to be, my Lord, Your obedient servant
His wife:	The Most Honble The Marchioness of C——
Begin:	Madam

MASTER OF THE ROLLS	The Right Honble The Master of the Rolls
Begin:	My Lord
or	Sir

MASTER (Scottish) See page 65.

MASTER (of a college) The principals of colleges in universities are variously styled Master, President, Principal, Warden, Rector, Dean, Provost, Censor or Director. He should be addressed accordingly, as

	The Master of B—— College, The University of C——
Begin:	Sir *or* Dear Sir

MAYOR (of a Borough)	The Worshipful The Mayor of D——
or	His Worship the Mayor of ——

If he or she is mayor of a *city* of which the chief citizen has *not* been accorded the prefix 'Right Honble' the envelope address is: The Right Worshipful the Mayor of E——

Begin:	Sir (or Madam, if the mayor is a woman)

Only when a mayor is sitting in court as a magistrate should he, or she, be addressed as 'Your Worship'.

METROPOLITAN (of the Eastern Church)	His Beatitude The Metropolitan of A——
Begin:	Your Grace
End:	I am, Sir, Your Grace's obedient servant

MINISTERS (of Religion: see CLERGY)
          (diplomatic: see ENVOY)

MONSIGNOR This form of address, or its Italian form
Monsignore (plural Monsignori) is applied to several higher
ranks of the Roman Catholic clergy.

OFFICERS Letters to officers of the armed forces—and,
generally, to retired officers of and above the rank of Captain
in the Army (and equivalent rank in other services)—bear their
rank on the envelope and in the Direction. The military rank
is placed in front of any other title, thus:

> Field Marshal The Right Hon.
> The Earl of A——, KG, &c.

or

> Major Sir John Smith-Brown-
> Smith, Bt.

In the case of naval officers, the letters RN follow the name,
or any initials of orders or decorations that appear after the
name, thus:

> Captain J. B. Smith-Brown,
> CBE, RN.

Retired naval officers usually place RN (retd) after the
name; and Royal Marines officers add RM.

The Salutation, or Greeting, is:

> Dear Major Jones,

or

> Dear General Robinson,

or

> Dear Group Captain Reed.

But if 'General Robinson' is 'General Sir Richard Robinson', begin as for a knight, without the military rank:

> Dear Sir *or* Dear Sir Richard

Officers below the rank of Captain in the Army (and its
equivalents) are not addressed by their military rank. Salute
as

> Dear Mr Green

Officers of the women's services are addressed by their
military rank in the same way, on the envelope and in the
letter; or, alternatively, as 'Madam'.

A table of equivalent ranks of commissioned officers in the Armed Forces and women's services is on page 149.

POPE (head of the Roman Catholic Church)	His Holiness The Pope
Begin:	Your Holiness
or	Most Holy Father
End:	I have the honour to remain Your Holiness's most devoted and obedient child
or	Your Holiness's most humble child

A non-Catholic might suitably end a letter to the Pope:

> I have the honour to be, Your faithful servant

PREBENDARY	The Revd Prebendary J. S——
Begin:	Reverend Sir

PRIEST: clergy of the Roman Catholic Church, and some Anglicans, are styled 'Reverend Fathers', which may be written 'Rev. Fr.'. They are addressed as 'Father'.

PRIMATE (see ARCHBISHOP)

PRIME MINISTER	The Rt Hon. J—— K——, MP, Prime Minister, 10 Downing Street

(or the official residence in the country concerned)

Begin:	Sir
End:	I am, Sir, Yours faithfully

PRINCE and PRINCESS (see ROYALTY)

PRINCIPAL (see MASTER)

PRIVY COUNCILLOR	The Right Honble L—— M——
Begin:	My Lord (if a peer) or Sir

Membership of the Privy Council is an office, although it is sometimes conferred as an honour or reward for good services. It may be held by a peer, baronet, knight or commoner, or a woman who is or has been a member of the Cabinet; it is held for life, and the prefix 'Right Honble' is used for life (*ie*, after retirement from any office). It is not hereditary, and confers no honour or prefix on the wife (or husband) of a privy councillor.

The prefix precedes the 'Sir' of a baronet or knight; but any military (&c.) rank held precedes the prefix; *eg*, 'Major General The Right Honble Sir John S——'. The letters PC should not be used after the name unless he is a peer.

PROVINCIAL	The Very Revd Father Provincial
or	The Very Revd Father J——
Begin:	Very Revd Father

He is the head of a Roman Catholic religious order, the initials of which should be placed after his name on an envelope, as SJ *or* OSB, &c.

PROVOST There is no special form of address for a letter to a provost. (The Scottish equivalent of Mayor).

QUEEN (see beginning of this section; also ROYALTY)

RABBI	The Revd Rabbi B—— C——
Begin:	Revd and Dear Sir

RECTOR (of church—see CLERGY)
       (of College—see MASTER)

ROYALTY The forms that are proper in addressing, beginning and ending a letter to Her Majesty the Queen have been given at the beginning of this section.

A letter to the Queen Mother would be begun and ended in exactly the same terms, and addressed

> To Her Majesty Queen Elizabeth
> The Queen Mother.

Letters to Princes and Princesses (of the British Royal Family) should begin:

Sir (*or* Madam)

but should end: I have the honour to be, Sir (or Madam),
Your Royal Highness's most humble and obedient servant

The form of address on the envelope will vary according to the individual. At the time of writing this, they are as follows:

His Royal Highness The Prince Philip
  Duke of Edinburgh, KG, &c.

His Royal Highness the Prince of Wales, KG

Her Royal Highness the Princess Anne

Her Royal Highness the Princess Margaret,
  Countess of Snowdon, CI, GCVO

Field Marshal His Royal Highness The Duke of Gloucester,
  KG, &c.

Her Royal Highness The Duchess of Gloucester, CI,
  GCVO, GBE

His Royal Highness The Duke of Kent, GCMG, GCVO

Her Royal Highness The Duchess of Kent

Her Royal Highness The Princess Alexandra, the Hon.
  Mrs Angus Ogilvy, GCVO

His Royal Highness the Prince Michael of Kent

Her Royal Highness The Princess Alice,
  Countess of Athlone, VA, GCVO, GBE

His Royal Highness The Prince William of Gloucester

His Royal Highness The Prince Richard of Gloucester.

The sons of the late Princess Royal are not Royal Highnesses and are addressed according to their rank: the elder as an earl, the younger as an earl's younger son.

VICAR (see CLERGY)

VICE-CHANCELLOR	The Vice-Chancellor of the University of C——
VISCOUNT	The Rt Hon. The Viscount N——
(informally)	Lord N——

Begin and end as for BARON (see earlier this section). His wife is 'The Viscountess N——' and his sons and unmarried daughters are 'The Honble John (or Joan) Brown' (or whatever the family surname may be).

WOMEN OFFICERS (see OFFICERS)

(FORMS OF ADDRESS IN THE U.S.A.)

AMBASSADOR	The Hon. J—— B—— US Ambassador in ——
Begin:	Dear Mr Ambassador
CABINET OFFICERS	The Hon. Mr J—— B——, Secretary of (Defense, Labor, &c.) Dear Mr Secretary,
CHIEF JUSTICE	The Chief Justice of the United States, US Supreme Court Building, Washington, DC Dear Mr Chief Justice,

An Associate Justice of the US Supreme Court is addressed Dear Mr Justice,

GOVERNOR	The Hon. C—— D——, Governor of New York State,
or	Governor C—— D——, State House, Albany, NY. Dear Mr Governor,
JUDGE	The Hon. E—— F—— Associate Judge, US District Court, —— Dear Judge F——,

MAYOR	The Hon. G—— H——, Mayor of N——,
or	Mayor G—— G—— City Hall, —— Dear Mr Mayor,

PRESIDENT	The President
	   The White House,
	      Washington, DC
	Mr President,

or	Dear Mr President,
REPRESENTATIVE	The Hon. J—— J——
or	Representative J—— J——, House of Representatives,

Note: The form of address is the same for Members of State Legislature as for those of the Federal Congress. A Representative should never be addressed as 'Congressman'.

SENATOR	The Hon. L—— M——,
	   US Senate,
	      Washington, DC

or	Senator L—— M——, Dear Senator,
VICE-PRESIDENT	(as for the President)

4

LETTERS FOR VARIOUS OCCASIONS

ANYONE WHO takes the trouble to read and understand what has been written in this book on grammar and syntax, the different parts of a letter and the ways of employing them, should be well enough equipped to write a letter to anyone on any subject or occasion. With a good English dictionary in case there is need to check the spelling or the meaning of a word, and attention to handwriting or typing so that the letter shall be neat, clear and pleasing to the eye, letter writing should present few difficulties.

ANNOUNCEMENTS

Note: A handwritten letter is much more human, friendly and flattering to the recipient than a printed form.

1

Dear Stanley,

I'm delighted to tell you that I have just become engaged. I think you will remember my fiancée, Jane S——, from the days when you used to live here.

We are only having a short engagement, and an invitation to the wedding will reach you very soon. I do hope that you will be able to come.

Yours sincerely,
John.

2

My dear James,

I am sure you will be interested to hear that I am going to marry again. Since Louise's death I have been very lonely, and although I shall never forget her I feel she would not wish me to be without companionship for the rest of my life.

My fiancée, Mrs Helen J——, was widowed two years ago, and now wants to make a new life. I am sure we are going to be very happy and I wanted you to be the first to know of the wedding. We plan to be married quietly on June 2, and of course I hope very much that you will be able to come.

Yours ever,
Michael.

3

Dear Susan,

I feel sure that you will be interested to know that I am going to be married on April 2, and I hope that you will be able to come along and give me your support.

My bride will be Mary B——, whom I do not think you have yet met, but I am sure you will think I am very lucky when you do meet her.

Her parents will be sending out the invitations shortly, and I hope that you will be able to come. Wish me luck, anyway, please!

Yours sincerely,
Nigel.

4

Dear Daphne,

This is to let you know that I am going to be married on May 1, and I do hope that you will be one of my bridesmaids.

Yes, I am marrying John D—— and he is such a dear that I am sure we are going to be very happy.

Do come round tomorrow evening, and we can have a good long talk about it. John and I (&c., &c.).

Yours affectionately,
Jane.

5

Dear Philip,

I am sure you will be glad to hear that we have a son, born at one o'clock yesterday morning. He weighed nine pounds, one ounce. Patricia and our son (and I!) are doing well.

We have not yet decided what to call him, but we both hope that you will be one of his godfathers when the time comes for his christening. As one of his names we have a fancy for your own second name, David.

Patricia will be home next week and then you must come and see us all.

Yours ever,
Tony.

6

Dear Mr Brown,

I am sorry to have to tell you that my father died quite peacefully yesterday, after a mercifully short illness. I hope and believe he suffered very little pain, but as you know he was a man who never complained.

The funeral will be at —— on —— and we shall see you then if you find it possible to come.

Yours sincerely,
John Richards.

CONDOLENCE

7

Dear Arthur,

I am very sorry to hear of the death of your wife, my cousin, and Elizabeth and I offer you our sincere sympathy.

Although we only saw each other occasionally during recent years we spent a good deal of our childhood together, and I have many pleasant memories of those days. I know how very happy my cousin was in her marriage to you.

If we can help you in any way do please let us know immediately.

Yours very sincerely,

Edward Cooke.

8

Dear Mrs F——,

All of us in the office were deeply sorry to hear of your bereavement. Your husband was the friend of all of us here, and a man whom we greatly admired, as well as liked, for his sterling qualities and his good comradeship.

He was always so even tempered, so helpful to newcomers, so ready to take his full share of the work of the office, that he won the regard of all of us, and each of us feels he has lost a true friend.

But your loss of a husband is infinitely greater than our loss of a loyal colleague, and I have been asked by your husband's office friends to convey to you our deepest sympathy with you and your family, and to say that if there is anything we can do to help you, we hope that you will not hesitate to let us know.

Yours very truly,

Keith B. S——.

9

Dear Mary,

I was exceedingly sorry to hear of the tragic passing of your dear husband, who was my friend for a great many years, ever since we were at school together. He had many fine qualities, not least his rich sense of humour and his high sense of honour, which endeared him to a very wide circle.

We have all lost a good friend, but your loss is so much greater than ours can be that it is difficult to know just what one can say. You may be sure that the heartfelt sympathy of myself and many of his friends is entirely yours. If there is anything that any of us can do to help you, we shall be glad to try.

At least you will know that you have the sympathy of all of us to help to sustain you in your loss.

Yours sincerely,

Cynthia.

10

Dear Mrs G——,

I am instructed by the Board of Directors to convey to you the deep sympathy of the Board, and indeed of the whole Company, in the loss you have sustained by the passing of your husband.

He was a highly valued employee of this Company, to which he had given so many years of loyal and devoted service, and he was held in great regard by the Board of Directors, his office colleagues, and also many of the Company's customers, for the quality and integrity of his work and his personal character.

We shall see that arrangements are made for the Board to be represented at the funeral of your husband, as soon as you can let us know where it is to be.

I hope that you will not hesitate to write to me if there is any immediate difficulty in your circumstances in which the Company might be of assistance to you.

Yours very truly,

B. G. P——.

Secretary to the Board
of Directors.

CONGRATULATION

11

Dear Christopher,

Hearty congratulations on your marriage! I wish I could have been at your wedding, but I have only just arrived back in England. I am sure that you are very lucky, and I look forward to meeting your wife soon and offering her my sympathy!

But seriously, I am very pleased to know that you have decided to get married at last, and I do wish you, and your wife, the very best of good luck in the many years together which I hope will be yours.

With every good wish,

Yours ever,

Roger.

12

Dear Sally,

All of us at D—— & Co.'s were delighted to hear of your marriage, and we wish you all the best of good luck and many years in which to enjoy it!

You kept it all very dark and we did not hear of the arrangements in time to make you a present beforehand; but we have subscribed to send you this little gift, which we hope you will find a place for in your new home. It comes from all of us with our most cordial good wishes to you both.

Yours sincerely,

Gillian.

13

Dear Jim,

Congratulations on the arrival of your son and heir! We were delighted to hear the good news, and especially to know that Jennifer and the new arrival are both well.

. What are you going to call him? We look forward to seeing him as soon as possible. Meanwhile, take care of yourself. We are sure you are going to make a wonderful father, but don't get too excited about it!

Congratulations again, and please give them to Jennifer when you see her, from both of us.

Yours sincerely,
Peter.

14

Dear Jonathan,

Our heartiest congratulations on winning the scholarship! A wonderful show. Your mother and I sent you a telegram yesterday—which I hope you got—and when you come home we will have a real celebration party. Later we shall have to go into the question of ways and means, but don't worry about that at the moment.

I don't mind saying now, old boy, that I have really admired the way you have stuck to your work during the past year. Your success now is the reward.

Always your affectionate
Father.

BOOKING ACCOMMODATION

Here are some specimen letters which might be written to book accommodation of one sort or another:

1

The Manager,
Blank Hotel,
Norwich.

Dear Sir,

I shall be in Norwich on business for two days next week, arriving on Tuesday morning, May 23. I shall be obliged if you will reserve one single room for me for that night.

If you cannot meet my need, please be so kind as to pass this letter on to some other first-class hotel which you think might be able to accommodate me.

Yours faithfully,
(*signature*)

2

The Proprietress,
Sunnylands Guest House,
Avenue Road,
Worpington-on-Sea.

Dear Madam,

Mr Burnham, who is a colleague of mine in business, tells me how happy he and his family were when they stayed with you last year. I am writing therefore to know if you would have accommodation for my wife and myself, and our three children aged 9, 6 and 2, for a fortnight in July this year. At the moment the exact two weeks we come do not matter so I leave it to you to make suggestions.

We should require two rooms, one for the two elder children and the other for ourselves. The baby can sleep with us if you can provide an extra bed in our room.

I would be grateful if you would quote me your terms for full board, and I hope very much you will be able to fit us in.

Yours truly,
(*signature*)

3

The Manager,
Blank Hotel,
Deal.

Dear Sir,

My wife and I propose to spend three weeks' holiday in Deal from Saturday July 3, and I shall be glad to know if you will be able to accommodate us, as —— have recommended your hotel to me most warmly.

We shall be driving down and I should require garage accommodation for my car. My wife's asthma necessitates our having a bedroom and sitting-room on the first floor, as near to the lift as possible.

I hope very much to hear you can fit us in.

Yours faithfully,
(*signature*)

4

The Manager,
Blank Steamship Co., Ltd,
(address)

Dear Sir,

I want to book two first-class passages to Montreal, for my wife and myself, and I should be glad if you will let me know what accommodation is available in the *Queen Anne* sailing on May 1, from Southampton; also what it all costs.

If the *Queen Anne* is already fully booked, kindly let me know what is the first ship by which you could book us, and its date of sailing.

Yours faithfully,
(*signature*)

5

Messrs X & Y,
Estate Agents,
(address)

Dear Sirs,

I want to rent a furnished house in Devon or Cornwall for the whole month of August, and I shall be obliged if you will send me particulars of any that you have on your books.

The house must have at least three bedrooms, a modern kitchen, good sanitation and mains water. I am not particular about electric lighting, or telephone. We want a quiet holiday well outside any town, but with facilities for food deliveries.

There are three of us—my wife, my son aged 15, and myself. The house must be within easy reach of the sea, and have a garage or some sort of covered accommodation for my car.

I should be willing to pay up to £— for the month.

Yours faithfully,
(*signature*)

INVITATIONS

Dear Geoffrey,

We are having a small party next Saturday to celebrate our tenth wedding anniversary, and we shall be so glad if you and your wife will join us here at about 7.30 p.m. Come as you are, and we will have a quiet game of Bridge after a meal.

Yours sincerely,
Joan and Edward Smith.

Dear Johnson,

We wonder if you and your wife can dine with us on Saturday 21st, when we are having a small party to celebrate my wife's birthday. Come along at 7.15. Dinner jacket; dancing or Bridge afterwards.

We do hope that you will both be able to come.

Sincerely yours,
Graham Lynn.

This sort of informal invitation does not call for any formal reply, but a brief note expressing thanks and saying 'We shall be delighted to come on Saturday' is enough to let the hosts know how many guests to arrange for, and to check the date.

Invitations of a formal or semi-formal kind usually have the initials RSVP at the foot. These are the initials of four French words (*Répondez, s'il vous plaît*) which mean 'Reply, if you please'. They have become fixed in the English language as the conventional form of asking for an answer to any invitation.

The formal or semi-formal style of invitation which is customary is the 'Third Person' style ('Person' in grammar is dealt with in Section 6). This is the form generally used for wedding invitations, which are sent out by the bride's parents, usually in this manner:

Mr and Mrs J. T. Smith request the pleasure of Mr and Mrs T. J. Brown's Company at the Marriage of their only daughter, Hilary Olivia Smith, to Mr George Hugh Robinson, which will be celebrated at St Paul's Church, Queensferry Road, Northampton, on Saturday September 3, 19— at 12 noon; and afterwards at the Imperial Hotel.

RSVP
   Glenlivet,
     Perth Road,
      Northampton.

This sort of wedding invitation is often obtained from a local stationer (die-stamping to be used for choice), with a blank space in which the name of the guest or guests is filled in by the bride's mother. An invitation in Third Person style should be answered in the same way, whether you accept or refuse it. Thus:

Mr and Mrs T. J. Brown thank Mr and Mrs J. T. Smith for their kind invitation to attend the Marriage of Miss Hilary Olivia Smith with Mr George Hugh Robinson at St Paul's Church, Queensferry Road, Northampton, on Saturday September 3, 19— at 12 noon, and afterwards at the Reception.

Mr and Mrs T. J. Brown have much pleasure in accepting the invitation.

If, however, Mr and Mrs Brown do not wish, or are unable, to go to the wedding, their reply would be written in exactly the same terms except for the last sentence. This, instead, would read: 'Mr and Mrs T. J. Brown regret, however, that because of a previous engagement on that date they are unable to accept the invitation. They wish the young couple every happiness.' Or it might be 'because of Mrs Brown's illness' or 'their absence on holiday'.

It may be noted, too, that it is usual to send a wedding present if you are invited to a wedding, whether you attend the ceremony or not. The present should have enclosed with it a very brief note of good wishes, and bear the name and address of the sender. It should be addressed to the bride or the bridegroom, whoever is better known to the sender.

'THANK YOU' LETTERS

I

Dear Mary and Hugh,

I must write you a few words of thanks for a lovely weekend. It was a real rest and I enjoyed every moment of it.

I caught the train all right and here I am again in this depressing town wishing I were still with you. Once again all my thanks for a most happy time.

Yours very sincerely,
Graham.

2

Dear Michael,

Many thanks for the party last night. It was the greatest fun. How about having a twenty-first every year?!

The best of luck,
Yours sincerely,
Bill.

Alternatively, you may prefer to send a somewhat more formal letter of thanks to the parents who invited you; thus:

3

Dear Mr and Mrs Gray,

Thank you very much for asking me to Sylvia's twenty-first. It was a wonderful party and Sylvia looked lovely. You are very lucky parents!

Yours sincerely,
Nigel.

Acknowledgments of letters of congratulation present little difficulty in composition, as the following samples show:

4

Dear Aunt Jean,

Thank you very much for your kind letter congratulating me on winning a scholarship to Wadham.

I think I was very lucky, but it is most encouraging to know that other people think I did well.

I am looking forward to going up to Oxford in October, and I hope I shall continue to deserve the kind things you have written about me.

Your affectionate nephew,
James.

5

Dear Mr Oliver,

It was very good of you to write to congratulate me on winning the Gold Medal in the Poultry Show.

I am not sure whether I shall wear it before, or after, my other medals—for Gardening and Golf!

Anyway, it is good fun going in for these competitions, which someone has to win, and I was certainly very lucky. Thank you again for your kind letter. And I wish *you* 'better luck next time'.

Yours sincerely,
Charles Stewart.

Then there are the letters acknowledging messages of sympathy. Often so many letters are received that it is impossible to reply personally to everyone, and a printed letter has to be composed and sent instead. Some such form as this:

6

Mr and Mrs A. B. Young and Family return thanks for the very kind expressions of sympathy extended to them in their bereavement.

March, 19—

777 Wilton Street,
Bath.

An alternative style is to place at the top of the sheet the full name of the person who has died, with his (or her) dates of birth and death, and perhaps the words '*In Memoriam*' or the letters 'RIP' followed by some such letter as this:

Mr and Mrs A. B. Young and Family are very grateful for all the kind letters, and flowers which they have received. They especially thank you for your own message of sympathy, which is deeply appreciated.

March, 19—   777 Wilton Street,
                                              Bath.

ASKING FOR A LOAN

Dear ——,
        I hate to raise this matter with you, but you are the only person to whom I feel I can write in the circumstances. The fact is that due to unwise moves on my part in taking on too many commitments I am for the moment most embarrassed financially, and I am asking therefore if you could lend me £100.
        I promise you that I am taking immediate steps to free myself of nearly all these hire purchase agreements, which have been the main cause of the trouble, and in a few months I shall be straight. But I am most anxious, desperately so, to keep John at College and, as you know, I must continue to give £x a month to my mother.
        If you can help me, I feel I am on safe ground in saying I will be able to repay you the money by the end of next March.
        I don't think I need emphasise how much your help would mean to me. If you can lend me the money, I shall be in your debt long after the loan is settled—in fact for ever. If you cannot, I shall quite understand. Whatever the outcome, I hope it will not affect our friendship.

                                              Yours ever,
                                              ——

REFUSING A LOAN

Dear ——,
        I am very sorry to hear of your financial difficulties but I am so hard up myself that I just cannot lend you this money. I would most certainly help you if I were in a position to do so, but as things are I'm afraid it is quite out of the question.

                                              Yours sincerely,
                                              ——

Dear ——,

I am very sorry to hear of your financial difficulties but I am so hard up myself that I just cannot lend you this money, and I can only suggest that you throw yourself on the mercy of your bank manager. He is the best person to advise and help you.

Yours sincerely,

Dear ——,

I am very sorry indeed to hear of your financial problems. I have made it a principle never to lend people money; it is the royal road to losing friends. Here is £20 which I am truly delighted to give you. For the rest why not see your bank manager? If you explain to him all the circumstances and the steps you are taking to put matters right I am sure he will help you.

Yours ever,

LOVE LETTERS

It is certainly presumptuous and probably impossible to give examples of how to write these most intriguing of all letters—just remember always that every protestation made must be absolutely sincere, that promises of marriage in writing, unless really meant, are most ill-advised, and that a quarrel by post is usually irreparable. With these strictures well in mind, go ahead and enjoy yourself!

LETTERS TO EDITORS

Letters to newspaper editors are not paid for as contributions as a general rule, but they often make better reading than some of the newspaper's other contents. They are written by people who want to express their wants, ideas, needs or grievances publicly, and are printed because they are considered to be of wide general interest.

One may ask why some letters are published and others (the large majority) are rejected: there are many answers. One reason may be the letter's excessive length; a letter which would occupy a column or two will almost certainly be consigned to the editorial waste-paper basket. So, keep it short. Another reason may be its poor construction. If it takes several sentences to reach any recognisable point, it will lack reader-interest. So state the main point of your complaint, argument or suggestion in your first sentence.

Some magazines invite letters to be sent to the editor, and offer payment for those that are printed. Those containing complaints or queries are often followed by an editorial footnote explaining the reasons for the actions or situations they describe. Thus the 'feature' is helpful and informative to the whole readership.

Letters to the editor are not usually dealt with by 'the' editor, but are handled by members of the staff trained in this branch of newspaper production. Only on the smaller suburban or provincial newspapers does the editor deal personally with the letters, because he himself is the most experienced member of the journalistic staff: and letters can be dangerous for an editor if they contain libellous statements.

An editor has no right to publish a letter unless it is clearly intended for publication: and he is not entitled to publish the writer's name or address if he is requested not to do so. He will, however, always ask for the name and address of every correspondent, even if it is not for publication. It is regarded as a guarantee of the good faith of the writer; it enables the editor to pass on to the writer any replies to the letter he may receive—and also to get hold of the writer if any legal proceedings appear likely to arise.

LETTERS AND THE LAW

Some letters to editors cannot be published because they contain remarks that may be libellous. Actionable libel may be defined as the publication in writing or other permanent form of a false statement which tends to lower a person in the estimation of right-thinking members of society generally, or which tends to make them shun or avoid that person. If you write to an editor that 'Councillor —— is nothing better than a thief. He has stolen building material from the Council's stores to build himself a garage' no editor outside a mental home would print it. But even in writing it to the editor you have seriously libelled the Councillor (assuming your accusation was false), because 'publication' does not only mean publication in a newspaper: it includes making libellous statements about someone to a third party.

It is a serious matter to publish anything defamatory about someone else. If you do it, you may have to prove your statements are true: and saying is a very different matter from proving. In some circumstances even truth or a plea of justification might not succeed. For instance, you may know that ten years ago a prominent local man went to prison for six months for embezzling his employer's money. He *was* a thief: but it might be libellous if you brought the fact to the editor's attention now, ten years after the man's crime had been committed and punished, unless you were prepared to prove that the disclosure by you was a matter of public interest at that time and that you were not actuated by malice.

Moreover you may also be liable for damages if you make false and malicious statements as to anyone's title to. or as to, his property or goods, although such statements are not necessarily defamatory of the owner himself but nevertheless cause him damage.

As no publication is involved, you can write directly to anyone defaming him as much as you like and not caring whether your statements are true or false provided they are not of such an outrageous nature that a breach of the peace is likely to be created. However, in writing such a letter you should take care personally to write the letter and seal the envelope and mark it 'Personal and Private' and not dictate the letter to your secretary or typist. In fact similar precautions must be taken in regard to any letter you may write to any person containing defamatory statements about another in case you are unable to justify them. If you are really concerned as to someone else's acts or defaults your proper course was to sue him in the first place: not to write about him to other people.

From the above it follows that a complaint about some other person, whether sent to the head of a firm or to the editor of a newspaper, must be worded with the utmost care if an action at law is not to follow. Any form of disparagement of the honesty of a firm or individual should if possible be avoided.

Some people who write to editors have considerable talent for vituperation (or 'rudery') and will attack each other with strong words. There is no harm in doing that if malice and falsehood are avoided. A correspondent who is rude to another invites reprisals, and must not complain if he gets as good as, or better than, he gives. Provided the letters bear a fair and reasonable relation to the subject of the wordy battle an editor will allow wide latitude to the correspondents.

But a writer should himself avoid writing anything obscene, blasphemous, libellous, defamatory or knowingly untrue. The editor might be absent when the column is made up, a less experienced journalist may be in charge, and an action could result—and the action would lie against you, the writer, and also against the editor, the printers and the proprietors of the periodical in which your words appeared.

BUSINESS LETTERS

It has never been the intention of this book to attempt to give specimen letters for all possible contingencies. If this is attempted it invariably happens that the exact type of letter required, perhaps eagerly sought, is not to be found.

This book therefore does not attempt to tell you how to write to the local Council, an insurance company, a house agent, a lawyer, a banker, &c. What it does is to advise you not to be frightened through lack of experience when you have to write to any of these august people. Most of the same rules apply as when you were applying for a job—do a draft, and make sure you have put down everything you wish to say. Then see if it is in the right order, and so on. But above all, don't worry because you have no idea how to *phrase* some point which is technical or peculiar to the particular person or business to whom you are writing; just set down as clearly as is in your power what you are trying to get over—your recipient will understand and explain in the reply. Don't try to assume a greater knowledge than you possess. Innocence can be very disarming!

Note: Do make sure you have signed and dated the letter, and that somewhere your name and address are set down legibly.

RECORDS

A copy should be kept of all replies to private business letters to which it may be necessary to refer later; or at least a brief note should be pencilled on the received letter showing what sort of reply was sent, and when. These letters, and the copies of the replies, should be filed together if there is any likelihood that they will be needed in the future. Cheap files of the folder and clip, ring book or box kind, may be bought at any stationer's. Correspondence about one's income tax, house purchase, mortgage or lease, insurances, rates and other official dealings needs to be filed for reference, and copies of the replies sent should be filed with the letters received.

PAYMENTS

When paying duties on beer and betting (and certain other duties), one may obtain postal orders *free of poundage*, for sums not exceeding £50, on production at a post office of the official notice to pay.

POSTAGE

Some people think that there is no need to stick a stamp on a letter addressed to a Government department, or a Member of Parliament. This is wrong. It should be prepaid just as if it were addressed to a private person. Even a letter to a postmaster should bear the usual postage. It is only letters bearing the words 'Official Paid' (and usually 'On Her Majesty's Service' too) that may be posted without payment of postage.

No postage is payable on an address or petition to the Queen or to Parliament sent through a Peer or MP to either House of Parliament (provided it does not exceed 2 lb.).

If you wish to send an important letter without registering it, and yet be able to prove that you did in fact post it, you can hand it over the counter at a post office and ask for a certificate of posting. You will be charged a fee of 1p for this. The certificate can be used to prove that a particular letter (which may have been lost in transit or after delivery) was actually posted, and when it was posted. There is also the Recorded Delivery Service, which serves much the same purpose. Information can be obtained from any post office.

EXPRESSING LETTERS

Urgent letters which have missed the last collection from your own post office may be sent by train: what is called a Railway Letter. A letter, handed in personally at any railway station (except London Transport Executive stations and a few others) and properly stamped, will go by the first train to any other station, where it may be collected personally, or put into the letter box for the next local collection and delivery. (The charge for this Railway Letter service, in addition to the normal postal rate according to weight paid by ordinary postage stamps, is a railway fee the amount of which may be ascertained at any railway station booking office.) For all information about postal rates, &c., see the *Post Office Guide* (in Great Britain) or inquire at any post office.

COMMON GRAMMATICAL ERRORS

ERRORS IN syntax are committed every day, and the letter writer who wishes to write correctly may like to be warned of some of the commoner pitfalls. Reference may be necessary to Section 6 of this book.

First, the verb. A verb must agree with its subject in number and person. Here are some common errors caused by forgetting this:

(1) When plural nouns come between a singular subject and the verb: 'A snow-clad range of mountains, broken at intervals by steep passes, *extend* across the island.'—The subject is *range* (singular) so the verb should be *extends*.

(2) Two singular nouns or pronouns joined by *and* make a plural subject, requiring a plural verb; but joined by any other word or words, the first singular noun or pronoun is the subject, requiring a singular verb: 'The King and the Queen *were* there' but 'The King, with the Queen, *was* there'— 'The King, as well as the Queen, *was* there'—'The King, attended by his guards, *was* there'. But if the two nouns mean the same person or thing, the verb is singular: 'Your King and Conqueror speaks'.

(3) A collective noun is sometimes treated, wrongly, as singular in one part of a sentence and plural in another; as, 'The crew *goes* on board, and *they are* weighing anchor'.

(4) A plural noun which is the name of a single object needs a singular verb: '*The Arabian Nights is* a good book'— '*Gulliver's Travels* by Dean Swift *is* well worth reading'.

(5) Beware of the 'hanging nominative'—a term which means leaving a subject without a verb and passing on to a new statement.

Shakespeare's *Richard III* contains an example: '*They* who brought me in my master's hate, I live to look upon their tragedy'. *They*, with which the passage begins, has no verb to which it can be the subject, and the word is left in the air.

Another example: 'He considered that the committee's report, that the *exhaustion* of the mines, affecting the future of the whole country, was too serious to be disregarded'. What is the verb to which the noun *exhaustion* stands as subject?

(6) Where there are two subjects, one singular and one plural, to one verb, the form of the verb must agree with each of the subjects, and consequently must be used twice: *eg,* 'The post office *has been* broken into and the letters *have been* stolen'. (It is wrong to write: 'The post office has been broken into and the letters stolen'.)

(7) Transitive verbs, and prepositions, must be followed by the accusative case. The following examples are wrong; corrections in brackets:

Let you and *I* both go (write *me* for *I*).
Between you and *I*, he is wrong (*write me*).
Who are you talking about? (write *whom*).
Who do you mean? (write *whom*).
He invited my wife and *I* to dinner (write *me*).
Remember *who* you are talking to (write *whom*).

(8) Pronouns which form part of the predicate must agree with the word to which they refer: 'If I were *him*, I should write' (write *he*, to agree with *I*; the verb *were* can have no object).

(9) A relative pronoun must agree with its antecedent. There are several possible pitfalls. Examples of errors, with corrections in brackets, include: 'This is one of the fastest times that *has* been recorded' (write *have* to agree with relative pronoun *that*, the antecedent of which is *times*). 'In the end, after many struggles, he succeeded, *which* completely changed his outlook' (the relative pronoun *which* has no clear antecedent). 'This is the man *whom* the police think can help them' (write *who*—its antecedent is *man*, which is nominative case; *who* then becomes the subject of *can help* and must for that reason also be nominative).

(10) The conjunction *and* must not be used before a single relative clause, because a relative pronoun is itself a conjunction. But when there are two relative clauses referring to the same antecedent, the use of *and* before the second one is correct, although re-wording of the sentence may enable the writer to avoid it. Examples: (*wrong*)—'He was a brilliant writer, and who was also a skilful artist' (*who* is not required); (*wrong*)—'I boarded a ship having two masts and which had

only one funnel'; (*right*)—'He was a clever composer, whose works were often played, and whose reputation stood high.'

(11) Anybody, everybody, nobody, either, neither, each, every and none: These words, called distributive adjectives or pronouns, must be followed by verbs, pronouns and adjectives in the singular. Examples: Anybody who *comes* can write *his* name here (not *come*, or *their*). Everybody *writes* letters. Nobody could write *her* letter for the noise. Each boy will stamp *his* own letter. *Has* either of you seen my letter? Neither of you *has* any right to read it. Every singer *knows* the words. None of our men *is* missing. 'None but the brave *deserves* the fair.' (*Note: None*, or *no one*, is singular; but colloquially it is sometimes regarded as being equivalent to *not any* and used as plural.)

The pronoun *one* has the genitive case *one's*. It is wrong to write: 'One is proud of *his* own victory' (for *his* write *one's*).

(12) *Same* or *the same* should not be used as a pronoun, in ordinary writing, although both forms are used as pronouns in some legal documents, proclamations and prayers. This should be avoided in modern commercial and official correspondence. Use the personal pronoun or noun clause instead. Examples: 'With reference to the proposed sale, and my letter concerning *the same*' (substitute *it*). 'As you have not filled in your full Christian names, kindly *advise me of the same*' (write *tell me what they are*).

(13) In no circumstances should *like* be used as a conjunction. It is wrong to say or write: 'She does not cook *like* her mother did' (say *as*, or *as well as*).

(14) Errors in the use of *than* can be avoided by completing the sentence in which it is used. Examples: 'He has been quicker than *me*' is wrong; the completed sentence would be 'He has been quicker than I (have)' and *I* should be used whether *have* is added or not. 'She loves my mother more than me' is ambiguous as it stands. Does 'she' love mother more than she loves 'me' or more than I love mother? The sentence should be completed: either 'She loves my mother more than she loves me' or 'She loves my mother more than I do'. In the former of those two sentences there is a new possibility of misunderstanding: does the second *she* stand for the first *she*, or for *mother*? If for *mother* the sentence should be written: 'She loves my mother more than my mother loves me'.

These examples, and others in this book, show how careful

a writer must be, if his letter (or other writing) is to be perfectly clear to the reader.

(15) Many people spoil an otherwise well-written letter by leaving out necessary words, which makes for a slipshod appearance to their writing. For example, 'People have and still do argue about it' is wrong, because *argue* cannot follow both *have* and *do*; in effect, the sentence contains two sentences run together, and the verbs must be correct—'People have argued, and still do argue, about it'.

A similar, and commoner, error is to write: 'Jones is as good, or better than Smith'. The phrase *as good as* can be used only in its complete form to express the comparison: 'Jones is as good as, if not better than, Smith'.

Sometimes the omission of an auxiliary verb can upset the smoothness of a sentence; *eg*, 'The book which Jones had written and Smith published was the subject of the talk'. The past perfect tense *had written* must be continued with 'Smith *had published*' to make the sentence run smoothly and clearly.

(16) Sentences can be spoiled not only by omitting necessary words, but by placing the words in the wrong order in the sentence. Examples: 'He is *eager not only* to make money, but also anxious to keep it'—is wrong; say 'He is *not only eager* to make . . .' '*Either he was* right or wrong'—is wrong; say '*He was either* right or wrong'. 'Thinking *both* of money *and* power, he walked home'—is wrong; say 'Thinking of *both money and power*'. A moment's consideration of each of these examples will show why the one is wrong and the other is right.

(17) A common error is to confuse *less* and *fewer* when referring to numbers or quantities. 'I wrote no *less* than five letters' is wrong; it should be 'no *fewer* than five letters', because *fewer* refers to numbers and *less* to quantities. Similarly, *many* refers to numbers, *much* to quantities. The following examples are all correct: 'There were fewer than twenty members present.' 'His speech took less than an hour.' 'He has written many letters.' 'He has much good sense, and many good qualities.'

(18) Prepositions, prepositional phrases and bogus prepositions can cause errors if not understood. We hear radio announcers say: 'We apologise to listeners who missed the start of the programme, *due to* a technical fault in the transmitters'. Some grammarians maintain that *due to* should not

be used, as it is in that sentence, as a prepositional phrase; that *due* is an adjective and must have a noun to qualify. In the sentence quoted *due* does not qualify any noun: but it does if the announcer apologises 'for a *break* in the programme, *due to* a technical fault'. The break is (correctly) due to a fault.

'The delay in replying is due to the illness of my secretary' is correct; *due to* agrees with *delay*. 'There was no play today due to the rain' is wrong: *due to* cannot qualify *play*, or *no play*.

The usual substitute for *due to* in such sentences as the last, by those who try to be correct, is *owing to*, which has long been accepted as a prepositional phrase. But *owing to* is best kept for sentences in which there is some condition of indebtedness, of something actually being *owed*. We do not actually *owe* anything when we say that 'the delay was owing to a technical fault'.

The best prepositional phrase to use in these cases is *because of*, which immediately conveys the idea of *causation*. The *cause of* the delay was the technical fault; the lack of play was *because of* the rain. Nothing is *due* to rain; nothing is *owed* to rain. Rent can be due, and be owed; not rain. But rain can be a cause; so say *because of*.

Newspaper writers are largely responsible for the wrong use of *following* as a preposition, usually referring to something static; whereas it is correctly a verb, the present participle of *follow*, and obviously implies movement. Day follows night, and night follows day; a policeman follows a robber, and a car follows a road (*ie* moves along it). But it is surely nonsense to write: 'Following last night's heavy rain, the roads are flooded'. That simple little word *after* can usually be substituted for *following* in these misuses of a verb as a preposition. Other, sometimes more exact, substitutes are: because of, in consequence of, as a result of, in accordance with. But *after* is nearly always to be preferred.

(19) Mention of *after* brings to mind its 'opposite number' *before*, which is so often forgotten. Just as *following* is so often wrongly used for *after*, so is *prior to* so often unnecessarily substituted for *before*. There is no need for *prior to* as a prepositional phrase, and it sounds and looks pompous. *Prior* is a useful adjective, and it is correct to write of *a prior engagement*. It should not be used as a prepositional phrase, when it

becomes both unnecessary and unnatural. No one really thinks to himself 'Prior to eating my dinner, I shall take a walk', or 'He reached the door prior to me'. Be simple, and use *before*.

(20) It is often said that a writer should not end a sentence with a preposition. There is good warrant for doing so, in the Bible and in the works of many famous authors; and the best rule seems to be to avoid doing so if you can without so twisting your sentence that it becomes clumsy or even unintelligible, but not to hesitate to end with a preposition if that makes for clearer, more natural writing.

(21) Ordinary phrases are sometimes spoilt by the use of the wrong word: the substitution for a word of another which resembles it, or has a similar meaning, or belongs to another phrase. Here are some of these phrases: wrong ones on the left, correct ones on the right:

to doubt that . . .	to doubt whether . . .
to aim to do something	to aim at doing something . . .
in order that it can be done	in order that it may be done
wear a straight face	keep a straight face
to try and explain	to try to explain
on penalty of	under penalty of, *or* on pain of
keep in mind	bear in mind
become a prey	fall a prey
pronounce it as a failure	pronounce it a failure
style it as a barbarism	style it a barbarism
consider it as ended	consider it ended
accord a prize	award a prize
claim as being . . .	claim to be . . .
take objection to	raise an objection to, *or* take exception to
keep apace with the times	keep up with the times, *or* keep apace with changes
reduced to such a pitch	raised to such a pitch, *or* reduced to such a state
maintain's one's distance	keep one's distance
keep to his bed	keep his bed
he was refrained from	he was restrained from, *or* he refrained from
stamp it as being dull	stamp it as dull

6

REVISING YOUR GRAMMAR

THIS BOOK is concerned with letter writing, not with English composition in general, but many of those who may read it will have left school some time ago, and may wish to brush up their English grammar as an aid to good letter writing.

The following pages contain a much compressed résumé of English grammar, mainly in the form of definitions of terms used, and examples of how they are used. Much has necessarily been left out.

The foundation of all writing is

THE SENTENCE

A sentence is a group of words that makes complete sense. Or it may be defined as a complete thought expressed in words. It may consist of only one word, but then at least one other word, although not expressed, is 'understood' to be expressed; *eg*, 'Come!' which is really '(You) come!' A one-word expression, such as 'What?' is really 'What (is it)?' or 'What (do you mean)?'

The basic rule about a sentence is that it must contain a verb, either expressed or understood, because a verb is a word which says something about the person or thing concerned. A sentence may express:

> a statement—He is a good boy.
> a question—Is he a good boy?
> a command—Be a good boy!
> an exclamation—What a good boy he is!

A simple sentence consists of at least two parts: the subject and the Predicate.

SUBJECT: this is the word or words about which something is said by the word or words forming the Predicate.

PREDICATE: this is the word or words which say something about the Subject. The Predicate must contain a verb, expressed or understood.

In the first sentence above 'He' is the Subject, 'is a good boy' is the Predicate. The Subject is usually a noun or pronoun, but it may be a group of words which together form a Clause. Thus:

Girls sew. They sew.

Many of the older girls in the class were sewing.

Nouns, pronouns, verbs are three of the eight

PARTS OF SPEECH

The others are adjectives, adverbs, prepositions, conjunctions and interjections. These names are used elsewhere in this book, and must therefore be defined briefly here.

NOUN: the name of a person or thing. 'Thing' includes concrete objects (*eg*, table, loot), abstract qualities (*eg*, truth, beauty), places and people (London, Scotsmen), actions (murder, singing), and states (existence, death).

PRONOUN: a word used instead of a noun. The following italicised words are pronouns: '*We* spoke of John but *nobody* knew *him*, or knew *much* about *anybody* connected with either *us* or the *others*.'

VERB: a word which makes an assertion—which may be a question, statement, command, entreaty. A verb must always *say* something. No sentence is complete without a verb. A simple verb is one word: *eg*, *say*; a compound verb is more than one word: was saying, shall be saying, would say.

ADJECTIVE: a word used to qualify or further define a noun or pronoun; *eg*, *good* boy, *bad* girl, *the* Church, *Red* Indian.

ADVERB: a word which modifies a verb, adjective, another adverb, and sometimes a preposition, conjunction, or whole phrase or sentence. An adverb *never* qualifies a noun or pronoun. Examples: He is *well*. I am *very* glad. *There* you are. Go *today*.

PREPOSITION: a word used to join a noun or pronoun to another word to indicate some relation between them; *eg*, the tree *on* the hill; a pig *in* a poke; get *off* my foot.

CONJUNCTION: a word that connects words or groups of words; as, Jack *and* Jill. I came *because* you asked me.

INTERJECTION: a word expressing an emotion, or used as an exclamation: Oh! Ah! Damn! Good heavens!

Before giving further consideration to some of the Parts of Speech, here are other grammatical terms defined:

INFLEXION: a change of form in a word to express a change in its meaning or relationship; *eg, boy* and *boys*; *tall* and *taller*.

ACCIDENCE: that part of Grammar which enumerates and classifies Inflexions.

SYNTAX: the correct arrangement of words.

We have already defined two parts of a sentence: Subject and Predicate. The third main part of a sentence, although it is not always present, is the Object; and this may be direct or indirect.

DIRECT OBJECT: the thing on which the action expressed by the verb is directly exercised: Boy meets girl (*Boy* is subject, *meets* is predicate, *girl* is direct object).

INDIRECT OBJECT: a word denoting something affected indirectly by the verb's action, the person or thing to, or for, whom, or which, the action is done. *Eg,* I gave *him* money.

Besides the Sentence, which must contain a verb, there are other groupings of words that need to be defined and illustrated.

PHRASE; CLAUSE

PHRASE: a group of words, the equivalent of a single part of speech, not containing a verb; *eg,* 'He walked *in the garden*'— the italicised words form an *adverbial phrase* qualifying the verb *walked*.

CLAUSE: a part of a sentence which has a subject and a predicate of its own, but which cannot stand alone as a complete sentence (so they are called *subordinate clauses*). As with phrases, clauses are the equivalent of a single part of speech: they may be noun, adjectival or adverbial phrases, or clauses.

For example, in 'I will come *when I am ready*' the last four words form an adverbial clause qualifying the verb *will come*. The clause contains its own subject (the second *I*) and verb (*am*) but it is incomplete by itself.

Clauses depend for their meaning on the part of the sentence which makes the main statement ('I will come . . .'), but it is a mistake in writing a book or a letter to tack on a lot of clauses to one principal sentence. It is better to convert subordinate clauses into separate short sentences.

A complex sentence may consist of a main sentence or main clause, and several subordinate clauses. Thus: 'When I reached London/*I called on my uncle*/because he had often asked/ that I should visit him/whenever I could'. The main sentence is italicised; it is preceded by an adverb clause, and followed by an adverb, a noun and another adverb clause.

Brief attention must be given to the classifications of some of the Parts of Speech, to enable letter writers to use effectively the words which are their 'tools'.

NOUNS

There are two main kinds of noun: Proper, and Common.

PROPER NOUNS are the names of particular persons or things; John, York, Monday, June, England.

COMMON NOUNS are the names of each thing in a class of things of the same kind; boy, town, day, month, country.

There are several classifications of Common nouns: concrete, abstract, collective, verbal.

CONCRETE NOUN: the name of something solid: *eg*, man, house.

ABSTRACT: the name of a quality, condition or action: murder, manhood, sympathy.

COLLECTIVE: a word denoting a number of things taken together to constitute one thing: crowd, flock, army.

VERBAL: the name of an action: hunting, shooting, fishing.

The same noun may sometimes be Proper and sometimes Common. Thus: 'There were several *dukes* present, but the *Duke* of Ely was the tallest', where *dukes* is Common but the *Duke* is Proper.

Most nouns have inflexions (see earlier definition) to indicate Number, Case and Gender—terms which will now be defined.

NUMBER: everyone knows that Singular means one and Plural means more than one. The general rule for forming a plural from a singular form is to add -s, as: boy, boys, bee, bees. But there are many variations.

To a singular word ending in -s, -x, -ch, -sh or -z, add -es for the plural: miss, misses; fix, fixes; Jones, Joneses.

If the singular ends with Y after a vowel (*vowels* are the letters a, e, i, o, u) add -s: key, keys; money, moneys. But if the Y follows a consonant, change Y to I and add -es: lady, ladies; fly, flies.

The letters *qu* (which always go together in English) count as a consonant: soliloquy, soliloquies.

Proper names ending in Y always add -s: Mary, Marys.

If the singular ends with -f, -lf or -fe, change the F into V and add -es: leaf, leaves. Exceptions, where you just add -s and make no change of F, include: brief, chief, fife, grief, handkerchief, relief, strife. In some cases both plural forms are used: dwarf (dwarfs or dwarves), scarf, wharf, staff.

Most words ending in -o add -es to form the plural: potato, potatoes. Exceptions: piano, pianos; stiletto, stilettos.

Exceptional plurals are: brother, brothers or brethren; child, children; ox, oxen. Some plurals are formed by making a vowel change: foot, feet; louse, lice; man, men.

Brothers is used for members of a family: *brethren* for members of a society. Similarly, we have: cloth—*cloths*, for kinds or pieces of cloth: *clothes*, for garments; and the usual plural of fish is *fish*, but for a number of particular fish we use *fishes*. Like fish, we have two plurals for penny: *pennies* for several separate coins, and *pence* for a sum of money in these coins.

Dies are tools for stamping: *dice* are marked cubes for playing games. The singular of each word is *die*.

There are several words which have either no singular, or no plural, or have the same spelling whether used in the singular or the plural.

For example, *agenda*—the list of items for consideration at a meeting—is plural, and has no singular; so is *Saturnalia*, meaning an orgy or noisy revel.

Breeches and trousers, scissors and shears, pants and shorts, pliers and forceps, stairs—all these words look to be plural but are in fact singular and have no plural forms. When we need to refer to a plurality of any of them we usually put 'pairs of' before the word: 'two pairs of trousers'—'three pairs of scissors'.

Other nouns which are not used in the singular include mumps and measles; ethics, victuals and billiards; and geometrical *compasses*, although that word *is* the plural of the navigational instrument, the *compass*.

Series is both singular and plural: 'a series of plays'—'five series of plays'.

Note the two words *specie* and *species*. By *specie* we mean cash, as opposed to paper money, cheques, &c.; it has no plural form. *Species* means a kind or class, a sub-division of a genus in natural science; the word is both singular and plural —'the human species'—'four species are known'.

Another word which is both singular and plural is the French word *rendezvous* (pronounced 'rondayvoo') meaning a meeting place or assignation. For other foreign words and plurals see page 138.

Where nouns have the same spelling in the plural as in the singular meaning, it is only by the context that one knows which is intended. Examples are: sheep, swine, deer, grouse (the bird, not the grumble) and corps (meaning a body of men).

Some words expressing measure, number or weight use the singular form unchanged for their plural when they state a plural idea, but they are usually made into single compound nouns by hyphenation: *eg*, hundredweight, two-foot rule, three-year-old pony, five-year-old girl; 50 head of cattle, 30 beast.

Other words which look like plurals but are also singular nouns include: alms, eaves, riches, news. Another which looks plural but is not, is *summons*, the plural of which is *summonses*.

Compound nouns, whether written as one word, or hyphened, or used as separate words, usually form their plural by adding S at the end of the whole expression: *eg*, bandmasters, ne'er-do-wells, child welfare officers. But some inflect the first part, or both parts: *eg*, menservants, women-servants, sons-in-law.

When a compound consists of a noun and an adjective, the adjective is *not* inflected: this affects the formation of the plural. For instance, 'martial' means 'military' as in 'martial music', so a court martial is a military court; therefore its plural is *courts martial*.

Similarly, *Lord* is an adjective of courtesy in such styles as Lord Bishop, Lord Chamberlain, Lord Chancellor, Lord Justice, Lord Lieutenant, Lord President, Lord Privy Seal, Lord Steward; and other words preceding the noun are also uninflected in the plural—Lord Great Chamberlain, Lord Chief Justice, Lord High Steward.

In modern times most of these officers or officials are *not* lords (peers) but courtesy and tradition continue the honorific as a courtesy style. The plural forms are all made by adding S to the last word in each case: Lord Chamberlains, Lord Lieutenants.

The second word takes the S to make the plural, too, in such designations as Sea Lord, Vice-Chief, Field Marshal (note, only *one* L), Major-General, Lieutenant-Commander, Deputy Lieutenant, Lieutenant-General, Lieutenant-Colonel, Group Captain, &c.

CASE

The CASE of a noun or pronoun is its relation to other words in the sentence; and a noun or pronoun is said to be *in* a certain Case according to its relationship to those other words. There are five Cases.

NOMINATIVE: the Case of the subject of a sentence, and of any noun or pronoun referring to the subject. The following italicised words are in the Nominative Case: *I* said it. *Boys* and *girls* come out to play. *Mr Smith* is *manager*.

VOCATIVE: the 'addressing' case: *Sir*, what did you say? *Death*, where is thy sting? Come here, *John*!

ACCUSATIVE—the Objective Case, the Case of the direct object: Dogs bury *bones*. A noun or pronoun that is 'governed' by a preposition is also in this Case: Of *whom* do you speak?

Note that no part of the verb *be* can have an object; therefore the word on which its action appears to fall must be in the Nominative Case. That is why we should say, and must write, 'It is I' and *not* 'It is me' (*I* is Nominative, *me* is Accusative).

GENITIVE: the Possessive Case, denoting the possessor, owner or author of something; the only Case in English which is formed by Inflexion. A noun in the Genitive Case is *used* as an adjective to qualify a noun either expressed or understood.

The Genitive Case of a singular noun is usually formed by adding 's to it: all the King's horses; the cat's milk; the book is John's.

If the noun is plural but does *not* end with S, the genitive is formed in the same way: men's pipes; children's toys.

If the plural noun does end with S, the apostrophe is placed after it without an additional S: cut the boys' hair; soldiers' songs.

If a singular noun ends with S, the usual 's is generally added to form the genitive: St James's Palace; Dickens's novels.

But when the next word begins with S or an S sound, add only the apostrophe: for goodness' sake.

If the possessing word is of Greek or Hebrew origin, it is usual to add only the apostrophe: Socrates' teaching, Moses' law, in Jesus' name.

In compounds, add 's to the last part or word: the Lord Mayor of London's coach; my son-in-law's house.

DATIVE: the 'giving' case, the case of the Indirect Object; *eg*, in 'I gave it to him' *I*, the subject, is Nominative; *it*, the direct object, is Accusative; *him*, the indirect object, is Dative.

GENDER

Sex enters into our lives in many forms, usually pleasant; but the aspect of it which occurs in Grammar is pretty dull. It is called Gender. Fortunately, it is not nearly as important in English as it is in most other languages. There are four Genders: masculine, feminine, common, neuter.

Persons and animals, or the words representing them, which are of the male sex, are masculine; those of the female sex are feminine. Words which denote persons or animals which may be of either sex are of common gender: *eg*, child, parent, cousin, sheep, cattle. All other nouns, names of non-living things, are neuter: house, beer, meat.

Exceptions are the names of living things which are not ordinarily associated with sex, such as caterpillar, spider; and names of sterile animals, such as mule.

Although people sometimes refer to ships, motor cycles, engines, locomotives, as 'she' the words are really neuter. Similarly, where the idea of strength is present, as in the sun and the wind, we often use masculine pronouns; and where beauty, fertility or gentleness are implied, as in the moon, 'Mother' Nature, 'Mother' country, feminine words are used.

Differences of gender are shown in various ways:

(1) by different words—father, mother; cock, hen;
(2) by changing one part of a compound—manservant, maidservant;

(3) by adding a suffix (usually -ess) to the masculine word—baron, baroness; giant, giantess; or a foreign form—hero, heroine; executor, executrix.

PRONOUNS

Pronouns, words which stand instead of nouns to avoid frequent repetition, are divided into seven classes, the uses of which are indicated by the examples:

Personal:	I, we, they.
Possessive:	mine, ours, its.
Reflexive:	myself, themselves, oneself.
Demonstrative:	this, that, these, those.
Interrogative:	which? what?
Relative:	who, which, that.
Indefinite:	any, each, some.

PERSONAL: so called because they stand for all three PERSONS, a grammatical term, used thus:

First person:	the person speaking;
Second person:	the person spoken to;
Third person:	the person spoken about.

Personal, and also possessive, pronouns are inflected to show their case, as follows:

Case	1st Person		2nd Person		3rd Person	
	sing.	plur.	sing.	plur.	sing.	plur.
Nom.	I	we	thou	ye	he	they
			you	you	she	
					it	
Gen.	mine	ours	thine	yours	his	theirs
			yours		hers	
					its	
Acc. } Dat. }	me	us	thee	you	him	them
			you		her	
					it	

It is important to note that there is *no apostrophe* in any of the possessive pronouns: ours, yours, his, hers, its, theirs.

These Possessive Pronouns must be distinguished from six other words which look like them, but which are in fact Possessive *Adjectives*: my, our, thy, your, her and their. They cannot stand in place of a noun, but must be followed by a noun.

For example, we cannot say 'This is my'—we must say either 'This is mine' (pronoun) or 'This is my book' in which *my* is a Possessive Adjective.

It will be seen that the Possessive Pronouns are the Genitive Case of the Personal Pronouns with which they correspond.

RELATIVE Pronouns are pronouns which relate to some noun or other pronoun (which usually precedes it, and is called its antecedent). They also join clauses. Some of them are also INTERROGATIVE Pronouns, which ask questions. For example, in 'Who are you?' *who* is Interrogative; in 'I know who you are' *who* is Relative.

The pronoun *who* is inflected for case: Nom. *who*; Acc. and Dat. *whom*; Gen. *whose*. The following examples illustrate these uses:

I know who you are.	I know whom you saw.
Who attacked me?	Whom did you attack?
This is he of whom I spoke.	To whom do you refer?
Whose is this?	I know whose it is.
Give to him who needs help.	Give to whom you wish.
It is I whom you see.	It is I who speaks.

He is a man who, the police think, may be able to help them.

The following points about pronouns may be useful:

(1) The relatives are *who* (*whose*, *whom*), *which*, *that*, *what*, and sometimes *as* and *but*. *Who* relates to persons: *which* to animals or things: *that* to either persons or things: *what* to things only.

(2) Beware of excessive use of the Indefinite Pronoun *one*. It is possible to start a sentence with 'One knows well that one will be happy there, but . . .' and you get tangled up in a maze of 'ones'.

(3) Note the uses of the two compounds sometimes called Reciprocal Pronouns: *each other* and *one another*. They both denote an exchange of action: the old rule that *each other* is used of two things, *one another* of more than two, is no longer regarded as necessary.

(4) Note the difference between the pronoun *its* and the common contraction *it's*, which stands for *it is* or *it has*. The pronoun *its* has no apostrophe. The apostrophe in the contraction is a sign of omission, not of possession.

(5) No apostrophe is needed, either, in the Reflexive Pronoun *oneself*, which is a compound of *one* and *self*. It is wrong to write *one's self*.

(6) The Genitive Case of *who* is *whose*, which has no apostrophe. The word *who's* (like *it's*) is a contraction: it stands for *who is* or *who has*—Who's coming with me?—Who's been sitting in my chair?

VERBS

There are many classifications of verbs, which can be touched on only briefly here. A verb is called TRANSITIVE when it describes an action which is exercised directly on an object; and INTRANSITIVE when the action does *not* pass over to an object. Verbs are not invariably either one or the other, so we usually say that a verb is 'used transitively' or 'used intransitively', as the following examples show:

(1) Simple transitive verb: Boys *like* girls (If we say simply 'Boys like' we at once ask 'like what, or whom?' so there must be an object).

(2) Simple intransitive verb: the sun *shines* (It does not 'shine' anyone or anything, so no object is needed).

(3) Transitive verb with unexpressed object: She *reads* for amusement.

(4) Transitive verb of incomplete predication: this jam *tastes* good.

(5) Intransitive verb used transitively: Railways *run* goods trains.

(6) Intransitive verb used transitively with a preposition: He *laughs at* me.

Verbs 'of incomplete predication' are those which make no sense as predicates unless followed by another verb or other part of speech. 'This jam tastes' is meaningless unless we add a word or words; but when so used, they have no object.

CONJUGATION is the name given to the complete statement of the forms of a verb. These vary according to five functions, called: Number, Person, Voice, Tense, and Mood.

PERSON: defined under Pronouns; first, second and third.

NUMBER: also dealt with under Nouns and Pronouns.

A verb must agree with its *Subject* in Number and Person. *Eg*, I build; he builds; they build; he talks; men talk.

VOICE: the form of the verb which shows whether the subject acts or is acted upon; whether it performs, or suffers, the action. A verb is said to be in the ACTIVE VOICE when the subject performs the action: He won the race; and in the PASSIVE VOICE when the subject suffers, undergoes or receives the action: the race was won by him.

TENSE: the verb form used to state the time, continuance and completeness or incompleteness of the action. The following terms are used, as the examples show, to express the various tenses:

Present: I see
Past: I saw
Future: I shall see

The Continuous Tense forms of these tenses show that an action still goes on: I am seeing; I was seeing; I shall be seeing.

The Perfect Tense forms show that the action has been completed: I have seen; I had seen; I shall have seen.

The Conditional (or Future Continuing) Tenses imply another condition: I should see; I should have seen; I should be seeing.

MOOD: the form of the verb which denotes the manner in which an assertion is made. The three Moods are: Indicative, Imperative, and Subjunctive.

INDICATIVE Mood makes statements or asks questions: he goes; has he gone?

IMPERATIVE Mood gives commands or makes entreaties: Pray for me. Go now.

SUBJUNCTIVE Mood expresses a wish, concession, purpose, condition or uncertainty: God save the Queen; come what may; If that be so, I will go.

The parts of a verb are also classified as Finite and Infinite.

FINITE: a verb that makes a statement about something, and has its meaning limited by considerations of Person and Number, *eg*, The sun shines.

INFINITE: a verb that makes no assertion when used alone, and is unlimited by considerations of Person and Number. Infinite verbs include Infinitives, Participles, and Gerunds.

INFINITIVE: the verb with *to* before it, expressed or understood. We say 'the verb *to go*' and that is the Infinitive of that verb. Infinitives may be used like nouns (as a subject or object) or as predicates: *eg*, *To read* improves the mind. His pleasure *is to read* history books.

The Infinitive without *to* is used as the object of the verbs can, dare, do, may, must, need, shall, will. *Eg*, He can read. You may go. It is also used as a second object after the verbs feel, hear, make, see. *Eg*, He made me go.

GERUND: the verb part ending with -*ing* which is used as a noun: as subject or object of a verb, or qualified by an adjective, or governed by a preposition. Examples: *Reading* improves the mind. I regretted his *going*. He spends his time *in talking*. His *coming* made all the difference.

PARTICIPLES are of two kinds: Present and Past. Present Participles (like Gerunds, with which they are often confused) end in -*ing*: Past Participles usually end in -*ed* or -*t*. The distinction between a Present Participle and a Gerund depends on the function performed by the word in its context: participles act as verbs, gerunds as nouns; but both sometimes as other parts of speech.

The following special points should be noted:

(1) A double or multiple subject takes a plural verb; *eg*, The writer and I *are* friends. But when the two parts of a double subject are so closely connected that they express only one idea, the verb may be singular; *eg*, The whole *aim and object* of a letter *is* to convey ideas.

(2) If the subject consists of two or more singular words with *either . . . or*, or with *neither . . . nor*, the verb is singular; *eg*, Neither he nor his son *writes* to me. But if the second subject is plural, the verb must be plural; *eg*, Neither he nor his brothers *write* to me.

(3) The verb agrees with the nearer of two or more subjects, in Person as well as in Number, when they are similarly separated; *eg*, Neither his brothers nor I *am* going to write to him.

(4) A Collective Noun takes either a singular or a plural verb, according to what is intended: *eg*, The Cabinet *has* decided to amend the law; The Cabinet *are* divided about amending the law.

(5) A Gerund is a noun and requires to be preceded by a word in the Genitive, or Possessive case; *eg*, I regretted his going (*not* him going); He said that John's coming might help (*not* John).

7

PROPER PREPOSITIONS

MANY MISTAKES are made in the choice of preposition to follow a particular word, especially a verb or a word possessing verbal force. The following is a list of correct prepositions:

abandoned, *to, by,*
abate, *of*
abhorrence, *of*
abhorrent, *to*
abide, *at, by, in, with*
abominable, *to*
abound, *in, with*
abridge, *from*
absent, *from*
abstain, abstinence, *from*
abut, *on*
accede, *to*
acceptable, *to*
access, *to*
accessory, accessary, *after, before, to*
accommodate, *to, with, in*
accompanied, *by, with*
accord (intrans.), *with*
(trans.), *to*
accordance, *with*
according, *to*
account, *for, of, to*
accountable (person), *to*
(thing), *for*
accuse, *of*
acquaint, acquaintance, *with*
acquiesce, *in, to*
acquit, *of*
adapt, *to*
add, *to*
address, *to*
adept, *in, at*
adequate, *to*
adhere, *to*

adjacent, *to*
adjourn, *at, for, to*
adjudge, *to*
adjust, *to*
admission (access), *to*
(entrance), *into*
admit, *of, to*
admonish, *against, by*
advantage, *of, over*
adverse, *to*
advise, *of, to*
advocate, *for*
affinity, *between, to, with*
afraid, *of*
agree (person), *with*
(proposal), *to*
(plans, conditions), *upon*
agreeable, *to*
aim, *at*
alienate, *from*
allude, *to*
alteration, *in, to*
ambitious, *of, to*
amenable, *to*
analogous, *to*
analogy, *between, to, with*
angry (person), *with*
(thing), *at*
animadvert, *on, upon*
annex, *to*
answer, *for, to*
antecedent, *to*
antipathy, *against, between, to*
anxious, *about, for, to (do something)*

apologise (person), *to*
     (act), *for*
apology, *for, to*
appeal, *from (one) to (another) for
     (help)*
appertain, *to*
applicable, apply, *to*
apprehensive, *of (danger), for
     (oneself)*
appropriate, *to*
approve, *of*
argue, *against, for (person,
     opinion),
     with (someone), on (a subject)*
arraign, *for*
arrange, *for (something), with
     (someone)*
array, *against (enemy), in, with
     (clothes)*
arrive, *at, in, with*
ashamed, *of, for*
ask, *after, for, of (person), to (a
     party)*
aspire, *to*
assent, *to*
assimilate, *to*
associate, *in, with*
assure, *of*
astonished, *at*
astride, *of*
atone, *for*
attach, *to*
attack, *on*
attain, *to*
attend, attentive, *to*
averse, aversion, *from, to*

ballot, *for*
banish, *from, to*
banter (someone), *for (something)*
bare, *of*
bargain, *for, with*
battle, *for*
bear (argument, event), *upon,
     with*
     (witness), *in favour of,
     against*

beguile, *of, with*
believe, *in*
belong, *to*
bereave, *of*
bestow, *on, upon*
betray, *to (someone), into (doing
     something)*
betroth, *to*
bigoted, *about, against*
bind, *to*
blame, *for*
blush, *at (oneself), for (others)*
boast, *of*
border, *on, upon*
born, *into (the world), of (woman),
     to (good luck)*
bound, *to, for*
brag, *of*

call, *at, for, on, upon*
capable, *of*
care, *for, to*
careful, *for, of*
careless, *about, of*
carp, *at*
catch, *at*
caution, *against*
certain, *of*
change, *for, with*
charge, *against, on, with*
clear, *for, from, of*
coalesce, *with, to*
coincide, *in, with*
comment, *on*
commit, *to, for*
common, *to (two or more)*
commune, *with*
communicate, *to, with*
compare, *to, with*
compatible, *with*
compete, *with, at*
complain, *of*
complement, *of*
comply, *with*
composed, *by, of*
concede, *to*
conceive, *against, of*

concerned, *at, for, about, with*

concur, *in, on, with, at*

condemn, *to*

condescend, *to*

conduce, *to*

confer (bestow), *on, upon*

confer (consult), *on, with*

confide, *in, to*

conform, conformable, in conformity, *to, with*

congenial, *to*

congratulate, *on, upon*

connect, *with, to*

conscious, *of*

consecrate, *to*

consent, *to*

consequent, *on, upon*

consign, *to*

consist, *in, of, with*

consistent, *with*

consonant, *to, with*

consult, *about, with*

contend, *against, for, with*

contradiction, *in, to*

contrast, *with*

conversant, *about, in, with*

convert, *into, to*

convict, convince, *of*

copy, *after, from*

correspond, correspondence, *to, with*

covered, *with, in*

cure, *of*

dash, *against, into, through, upon*

deal, *by, in, with*

debar, *from*

decide, *against, in favour of, on*

defend, *against, from*

defer, deference, *to*

defiance, *of*

deficiency, *of*

deficient, *in*

defraud, *of*

delighted, *at, in, to, with*

demand, *from, of*

denounce, *for*

depend, dependent, *on, upon*

deprive, *of*

derive, *from*

derogate, derogation, *from*

derogatory, *to*

descended, *from, of*

deserving, desirous, *of*

desist, *from*

despair, despoil, *of*

destined, *to*

destitute, *of*

detach, detract, deviate, *from*

devolve, *on, upon*

devote; dictate, *to*

die, *of* (disease), *by* (famine), *for* (person, cause)

differ, *from* (person, thing), *in* (some quality, opinion), *with* (someone)

difference, *between* (things), *in* (qualities), *on* (questions)

different, *from*

difficulty, *concerning, in*

diminish, *from*

diminution, *of*

disabled, *from*

disagree, *to, with*

disagreeable, *to*

disappointed, *in, with* (thing obtained, person), *of* (thing not obtained)

disapprove, *of*

discourage, *from*

discouragement, *to, with*

disengaged, *from*

disgusted, *at, with*

dislike, *to, for, of*

dismiss, *from*

disparagement, *to, of*

dispense, *with*

dispose, *of, for, to*

dispossess, *of*

dispute, *among, between, with*

disqualify, *for, from*

disregard, *of*

dissatisfied, *with, at*

dissent, *from*

dissimilar, *to*
dissuade, *from*
distinct, *from*
distinguish, *between, from*
distrustful; divested, *of*
divide, *between (two), among (more)*
dote, *on*
doubt, doubtful, *about, of*
dwell, *at, in, on*

eager, *after, for, in*
embark, *for, in, upon*
embellish, *with*
emerge, *from*
employ, *about, in, on*
emulous; enamoured, *of*
encounter, *with*
encouragement, *to*
encroach, *on, upon*
endeared, *to*
endeavour, *after, to*
endowed, endued, *with*
engaged, *for, in, on, with*
enter, entrance, *into, on, upon*
entranced, *with, by*
envious, *at, of*
equal, *with*
equivalent, *of, to*
estimated, *at*
estranged, *from*
exception, *against, from, to*
excluded, *from*
exclusive, *of*
expelled, *from*
expert, *at, in*
explanation, *of*
exposed, *to*
expressive, *of*

fall, *from, on, upon, under*
familiar, *to, with*
fawn, *on, upon*
fearful, *of*
feed, *on, upon*
fight, *against, for, with*
filled, *with*

fond, *of*
fondness, *for*
foreign, *to*
founded, *in (quality), on (fact)*
free, *from, in, of, with*
friendly, *to, with, towards*
frightened, *at, by*
frown, *at, on, upon*
fruitful, *in, of*
full, *of*
furnished, *with*

glad, *at, of*
glance, *at, over, upon*
glow; grapple, *with*
grateful, *for (favour), to (person)*
greedy, *of, for*
grieve, *at, for, over, about*
guard, *against, from*
guilty, *of*

hanker, *after*
happen, *on, to*
hardened, *against, by*
healed, *of*
hesitate, *to*
hinder, *from*
hiss, *at*
hold, *in, from, of*
hope, *of, for*
hostility, *to, towards*

identical, *with*
ignorant, *of*
immersed, *in*
impatient, *at, for, of*
impenetrable, *by, to*
impervious, *to*
impose, *on, upon*
inaccessible, *to*
incapable, *of*
incentive, *to*
incongruous, *with*
inconsistent, *with*
incorporate, *into, with*
independent, *of*
indifferent, *to*

indignant, *with* (*person*), *at* (*thing*)
indulge, *in, with*
indulgent, *to*
influence, *on, over, with*
inform, *about, of*
initiate, initiation, *in, into*
inquire, *about, after, for, of*
inroad, *into*
insensible, *of, to*
inseparable, *from*
insight; insinuate, *into*
insist, *on, upon*
inspection, *of, over, into*
instruct, *in*
intent, *on, upon*
interfere, intermeddle, *with*
intervene, *in, between*
intimate, *with*
introduce, *in, into, to*
intrude, *into, on*
inured, *to*
invasion, *of*
invested, *with*
irritated, *against, by* (*person*) *at, by*
    (*thing*)

jealous, *of*
jeer, *at*
join, *in, to, with*

knock, *at, on*
known, *to*

laden, *with*
land; laugh, *at*
lean, *against, on, upon*
level, *with*
liberal, *of, to, with*
liken, *to*
live, *at, in, on, with*
loaded, *with*
long, *after, for*
lord, *over*

made; make sure, *of*
marry, *to, with*
meddle, *with*
mediate, *between*

meditate, *on, upon*
meet, *with*
militate, *against*
mingle, *with*
minister, *to*
mistrustful, *of*
mix, *with*

necessary, *for, to*
need; neglectful, *of*
negotiate, *with*

obedient, *to*
object, *against, to*
oblivious; observant, *of*
obtrude, *on, upon*
obvious, *to*
offend, *against*
offensive; offer, *to*
operate, *on*
opposite, *to, of*
overwhelmed, *by, with*

parcel, *among, out*
parley, *with*
part, *from, with*
partake, *of*
partial, *to*
partiality, *for, to*
participate, *in, of*
passion, *for*
patient, *of, under, with*
paved, *with*
pay, *for*
peculiar, *to*
penetrate, *into, through*
persevere, *in*
pertain, *to*
pitch, *on, upon*
play, *on, upon, with*
pleasant, *to*
pleased, *with*
plunge, *into*
possessed, *of, by*
pounce, *on, upon*
pour, *into, on*
praise (*noun*), *for*

pray, *for, with*
predisposed, *to, towards*
predominate, *in, over*
prefer, *above, before, to*
preferable, *to*
preference, *above, before, over, to*
prefix, *to*
pregnant, *with*
prejudice, *against*
prejudicial, *to*
prepare, *for*
preserve, *for, from*
preside, *over*
press; presume, *on, upon*
pretence, *of*
pretend, *to*
prevail (persuade), *on, upon, with*
     (overcome), *against, over*
prevent, *from*
previous, *to*
prey, *on, upon*
prior, *to*
productive, *of*
profit, *by*
profitable; prone, *to*
pronouncement, *against* (person),
     on (thing)
propose, *to*
protect (others), *from*
          (oneself), *against*
protest, *against*
proud, *of*
provide, *against, for, with*
proximity, *to*
purge, *of, from*
pursuance; pursuit, *of*
pursuant, *to*

quarrel, *about, among, with*
quarter, *on, upon*
questioned, *by, on, about*

rail, *at*
reckon, *on, with*
recline, *on, upon*
recoil, *from*
reconcile, *to, with*

recover, *from*
reduce, *to, under*
refer, *to*
reflect, *on, upon*
refrain, *from*
regard, *for, to*
regret, *for*
regular, *in*
rejoice, *at, in, on account of*
relate, *to*
release; relieve, *from*
relevant, *to*
relish, *for, of*
rely, *on*
remain, *at, in*
remark, *on, upon*
remit, *to*
remonstrate, *against* (thing), *for*
     (action), *with* (person)
remove, *from*
repent, *of*
repine, *at*
replete, *with*
repose, *on*
repugnant, *to*
rescue, *from*
resemblance, *between, to*
resistance, *to*
resolve, *on, upon*
rest, *at, in, on*
restore, *from, to*
restrain, *from*
retire, *from, to*
rich, *in*
rid; rob, *of*
rove, *about, over*
rub, *against*
rule, *over*
rush, *against, on, upon, into, to, out
     of*

sated, satiated; satisfied; satu-
     rated, *with*
saved, *from*
seek, *after, for, to*
seize, *on, upon*
send, *for, to*

sensible, *of*
sensitive, *to*
sick; significant, *of*
similar, *to*
sink, *beneath, in, into*
sit, *in, on, upon*
skilful, *at, in*
smile, *at, on, upon*
snap; snatch; sneer, *at*
solicitous, *about, for*
sorry, *for*
stay, *at, in, with*
stick, *by, to*
strip, *of*
strive, *against, for, with*
subject; submissive; submit, *to*
subsequent, *to*
substitute, *for*
subtract; suffer, *from*
suitable, *for, to*
surprised, *at, by*
suspected, *by, of*
swerve, *from*
sympathise, *with*

tamper, *with*
taste, *for* (*something wanted*), *of*
  (*something possessed*)
tax, *for, with*
tend, *towards, to*

tendency; testimonial, *to*
thankful, *for*
think, *about, of, on*
thirst, *after, for*
tinker, *at, with*
touch, *at, on*
triumph, *over*
troublesome; true, *to*
trust, *in, to*

unison, *with*
unite, *to, with*
useful, *in, for, to*

value, *on, upon*
versed, *in*
vest, *in* (*person*), *with* (*thing*)
vexed, *with*

wait, *at, for, on*
weary, *of*
weep, *at, for*
witness, *to,* worthy, *of*

yearn, *for, towards*
yield, *to*
yoke, *with*

zealous, *for*

8

PUNCTUATION AND SPECIAL PLURALS

PUNCTUATION INCLUDES the use of CAPITAL letters, as well as the uses of the various punctuation marks. The rules for the use of Capital initial letters are as follows:

(1) New sentences begin with a capital.

(2) Proper nouns must have a capital (see Section 6).

(3) When you begin to quote what someone said, you must start the quotation with a capital, unless the quotation begins in the middle of a sentence.

(4) In writing letters each word of the Address, Direction and Salutation (terms defined in a previous section of this book) must have a capital. So must the Y of 'Yours faithfully' (or other Closing Phrase) but *not* the first letter of the second word ('faithfully' or 'truly' or 'very truly'). On the envelope, too, the initial letters of the person or company, and of each word of the address, must be in capitals.

(5) Titles of books, newspapers, magazines, plays, films, works of art, and trade names of goods should have capital letters for all the main words; but small letters for such connecting words as *the*, *of* and *and*, unless one of these is the *first* word of the title. *Eg*, write: *The Times* (newspaper), *News of the World*, *The Taming of the Shrew*, *The Memoirs of Sherlock Holmes*, *Woman and Home*.

(6) Titles of regiments and other military and air formations, names of ships, towns, countries, geographical locations (Spurn Head, Cardigan Bay), and initials that are contractions of proper nouns (for Knight of the Garter) or of compass directions (N-E for North-East) must have capitals.

(7) In poetry and songs each new line customarily begins with a capital, although in some modern verse the writer deliberately uses no capitals at all.

The uses of punctuation marks are to break up a narrative into understandable sections; to express to a reader the pauses, or the variations of tone, which would naturally occur if the narrative were being read aloud; to separate dependent clauses from main sentences, and sentences from each other, to divide from each other the items in a list, and in other similar ways to make the writer's meaning clear.

Punctuation marks used in English are: fullstop (.), colon (:), semicolon (;), hyphen (-), dash (—), single (' ') or double (" ") quotation marks, question mark (?) or query, exclamation mark (!) and brackets () or parenthesis. In letter writing we do not use many punctuation marks, but when we use them they should be used correctly. Only brief notes on their uses are necessary here.

Plenty of fullstops, which means short sentences, is a sound rule. This point has been stressed elsewhere in this book, but it cannot be emphasised too strongly that short sentences make easy reading, and very long ones can be boring or misleading. Every sentence, and every paragraph, must end with a fullstop, unless the wording requires the last mark to be a query, exclamation mark, or closing quotation marks.

The colon is used before the first item of a list of items; to set out something that is to be opposed by something else; and sometimes to introduce a quotation or dialogue. Examples: 'The contents of the room included: books, pictures, a piano, a model ship in a bottle, and two funny old gentlemen sitting by the fire.' 'He said that it was nonsense: I maintained that it was true.'

The semicolon marks a pause shorter than that indicated by a colon, longer than that intended by a comma. It is used to separate clauses in a sentence, or a series of parallel statements grouped into a sentence. It is not often required in a letter.

The comma, which marks a brief pause, is the commonest punctuation mark. In fact it is often used too frequently, both in letters and in print. It is used properly to separate the items in a list; two or more phrases qualifying the same word ('He had adventures by land, by sea, and by air'); to mark off words and phrases like: however, indeed, therefore, too, for instance, no doubt, in fact, of course; and sometimes to mark off between a pair of commas a phrase that is an interruption, an aside, or an explanation.

This last-mentioned function of the pair of commas is often done better by using brackets, or a pair of dashes. A single dash may be effectively used when you want to add something unexpected at the end of a sentence; eg, 'He expected a rebuke, but received a rise—lucky man!' The shorter hyphen unites the parts of compound words: mother-in-law, go-between. It is not needed in 'today', and similar words.

The question mark, query or note of interrogation should be used when a question is actually asked, but not when a question is only described. *Eg*, 'Who spoke?' asked John. John asked who spoke. The query is placed at the end of the sentence asking the question, and as it incorporates a fullstop in itself, no fullstop need be written in addition to the question mark.

Similarly, omit it with the exclamation mark, which is placed at the end of a sentence that describes something funny, exciting or surprising. It should not be used often.

The best way to grasp the uses and placings of punctuation marks is to study how they are used in books generally, and this book particularly.

SPECIAL PLURALS

The following words from other languages which have been adopted into English, form their plurals in either their original or in the English way:

singular	*meaning*	*plural*
addendum	something added	addenda
adieu	farewell	adieux, adieus
amanuensis	writer from dictation	amanuenses
analysis	reduction to elements	analyses
apparatus	appliance	apparatuses
aquarium	artificial pond or tank	aquaria (sci). aquariums (home)
axis	line through a centre	axes
bacillus	minute organism	bacilli (sci.) bacilluses (pop.)
bandeau	fillet binding girl's hair	bandeaux
bandit	outlaw, robber, gangster	banditti (outlaws) bandits (robbers)
base	bottom, support, start	bases
basis	foundation, beginning	bases
beau	lover, lady's man	beaux
bête noire	pet aversion	bêtes noires
chateau	country house	chateaux
conspectus	general view, summary	conspectuses

singular	meaning	plural
corpus	body, collection	corpora
corrigendum	thing to be corrected	corrigenda
cranium	bones of head	crania (sci.)
		craniums (pop.)
crematorium	place for burning bodies	crematoria, crematoriums
criterion	standard by which to judge	criteria
datum	thing known, or granted	data
dilemma	position allowing only a choice of evils	dilemmas
dilettante	amateur of Fine Arts	dilettanti
dogma	principle, Church doctrine	dogmata (Church)
		dogmas (pop.)
emphasis	intensity of feeling or expression	emphases
emporium	centre of commerce, shop	emporia, emporiums
encomium	formal praise	encomia, encomiums
exit (noun)	way out of building	exits
(verb)	he (or she) goes out (stage direction)	exeunt (they go out)
executrix	woman executor	executrices, executrixes
exordium	introduction	exordia
flambeau	torch	flambeaux, or flambeaus
forceps	surgical pincers	forcepses, or forcipes
formula	recipe, rule, set form of words, math. symbols	formulae (sci.), formulas
fungus	mushroom, toadstool, mould	fungi (sci.)
		funguses (pop.)
genius	spirit; creative person	genii (spirits)
		geniuses (people)
genus	group of animals or plants	genera
gladiolus	plant with spiky leaves	gladioli (sci.)
		gladioluses (pop).

singular	meaning	plural
hiatus	gap	hiatus, or hiatuses
hippopotamus	African river animal	hippopotami or, hippopotamuses
ignoramus	ignorant person	ignoramuses
index	mathematical term; list of references in a book	indices (math.) indexes (in books)
interregnum	interval between two reigns	interregna, or interregnums
lacuna	gap, cavity, missing part	lacunae (sci.) lacunas (pop).
medium	means of conveying ideas	media (esp. in advertising) mediums (esp. in Spiritualism)
memorandum	note to aid memory	memoranda, memorandums
metamorphosis	change of form	metamorphoses
miasma	fumes or gas from a marsh	miasmas, or miasmata
millennium	1,000 years; happy future	millennia
narcissus	flower, kind of daffodil	narcissuses, or narcissi
neurosis	nervous disorder	neuroses
nimbus	bright cloud, halo	nimbuses, or nimbi
oasis	fertile spot in desert	oases
octopus	eight-armed mollusc	octopodes (sci.) octopuses (pop.)
olympiad	4-year interval between Olympic Games	olympiads, olympiados
opera	dramatic play to music	operas
opus	musical work	opera
phenomenon	remarkable person or event	phenomena
plateau	elevated plain	plateaux, or plateaus
polypus	tumour (in nose)	polypi, polypuses
portmanteau	leather case for clothes	portmanteaux, or portmanteaus
prospectus	descriptive circular or book	prospectuses

singular	*meaning*	*plural*
purlieu	border, squalid area of town	purlieus
rhinoceros	African animal with horn on nose	rhinoceroses
rostrum	platform for speaker	rostra, or rostrums
rota	list of people, or duties	rotae, or rotas
rouleau	coil, roll, cylindrical packet of gold coins	rouleaux, or rouleaus
seraph	pure, celestial being	seraphim (Bible) seraphs (pop.)
spatula	broad-bladed instrument	spatulas
specie	coin (not paper money)	species
species	sort, kind, class of things	species
spectrum	image formed by light rays	spectra (sci.) spectrums (pop.)
stamen	plant organ holding pollen	stamens
stigma	brand, stain, imputation; religious marks on body	stigmas or stigmata
stratum	layer of deposit	strata
syllabus	course or programme of lessons	syllabuses
synthesis	putting together	syntheses
tableau	motionless group of people representing scene or event	tableaux
thesis	college exercise for degree; proposition in argument	theses
trousseau	bride's outfit of clothes	trousseaux
ultimatum	final proposal	ultimata, or ultimatums
vacuum	space devoid of matter	vacua, or vacuums
venus	goddess of love; lovely woman	Veneres, or venuses
viaticum	eucharist for dying person; portable altar	viatica, or viaticums
vortex	violent eddy, centre of a whirlpool	vortexes, or vortices

9

IDENTIFYING COUNTRIES

ADDRESSES ON letters from abroad, and the names of countries and territories that appear on their postage stamps, are often quite different from the names by which we in Great Britain know and refer to those countries.

Following is an alphabetically arranged list of countries with their English equivalent names; after which will be found a similar list with the English names first, in alphabetical order. Names which are the same are not included.

Açores	Azores
Africa Occidental Española	Spanish West Africa
Afrique Occidentale Française	French West Africa
Andorre	Andorra
Al Mamlaka al Arabiya as-Saudiya	Saudi Arabia
Belgie, Belgique	Belgium
Brasil	Brazil
Bulgariya	Bulgaria
Cabo Verde (Islas de)	Cape Verde Islands
Cambodge	Cambodia
Cameroun, République Fédérale du	Cameroon, Federal Republic of
Centrafricaine, République	Central African Republic
Ceskoslovenská	Czechoslovakia
Côte d'Ivoire, République de	Ivory Coast
Danmark	Denmark
Deutsche Demokratische Republik	German Democratic Republic (East Germany)
Deutschland, Bundesrepublik	German Federal Republic (West Germany)
Eire	Ireland, Republic of
España	Spain
Gabonaise, République	Gaboon Republic
Grønland	Greenland

Guiné Portuguesa	Portuguese Guinea
Guinée, République de	Guinea
Guinea Española	Spanish Guinea
Guyane Française	French Guiana
Hankuk	Korea
Haute-Volta, République de	Upper Volta, Republic of
Hellas	Greece
Helvetia	Switzerland
Iran	Persia
Island	Iceland
Italiana, Repubblica	Italy
Jugoslavije, Republika Federativna Narodna	Yugoslavia
Kampuchea	Cambodia
Liban	Lebanon
Magyarország	Hungary
Malgache, la République	Madagascar (Malagasy Republic)
Maroc, Royaume de	Morocco
Mauritanie, République Islamique de	Mauretania, Islamic Republic of
Mexicanos, Estados Unidos	Mexico
Moçambique	Mozambique
Nederland	Netherlands, Holland
Nederlandsche, Antillen de	Netherland Antilles
Nieuw Guinea	Netherlands New Guinea (West Irian)
Nippon Koku	Japan
Norge	Norway
Nouvelle Calédonie	New Caledonia
Nouvelles Hébrides	New Hebrides
Oceanie	French Oceania
Österreich	Austria
Pilipinas, Repúblika ng	The Philippines
Polska	Poland

Polynésie Française	French Polynesia
Portuguesa, Republica	Portugal
Romana, Republica Populara	Roumania
Sahara Español	Spanish Sahara
Schweiz	Switzerland
Shqiperise	Albania
Somalis, Côte Française des	French Somaliland
Suid-Africa, Republic van	Republic of South Africa
Suidwes-Afrika	South-West Africa
Suisse	Switzerland
Soyuz Sovetskikh Sotsialisticheskikh Respublik (C.C.C.P.)	Union of Soviet Socialist Republics (U.S.S.R.)
Suomi	Finland
Suriname	Surinam
Sverige	Sweden
Svizzera	Switzerland
Tchad, République du	Chad Republic
Thailand	Siam
Tunisienne République	Tunisia
Türkiye Cümhuriyeti	Turkey
Vaticano, Stato della Citta del	Vatican City State
Yisrael	Israel

* * *

Albania	Shqiperise
Andorra	Andorre
Austria	Österreich
Azores	Açores
Brazil	Brasil
Bulgaria	Bulgariya
Belgium	Belgie, Belgique
Cambodia	Cambodge; Kampuchea
Cameroon, Federal Republic of	Cameroun, République Fédérale du
Cape Verde Islands	Cabo Verde (Islas de)
Central African Republic	République Centrafricaine

Chad Republic	Tchad, République du
Czechoslovakia	Československá
Denmark	Danmark
Finland	Suomi
France	République Française
French Guiana	Guyane Française
French Oceania	Oceanie
French Polynesia	Polynésie Française
French Somaliland	Côte Française des Somalis
Gaboon Republic	République Gabonaise, Gabon
German Democratic Republic (East Germany)	Deutsche Demokratische Republik
German Federal Republic (West Germany)	Bundesrepublik Deutschland
Greece	Hellas
Greenland	Grønland
Guinea	Guinée, République de
Holland	Nederland
Hungary	Magyarország
Iceland	Island
Ireland, Republic of	Eire
Israel	Yisrael
Italy	Repubblica Italiana
Ivory Coast	Côte d'Ivoire (République de)
Japan	Nippon Koku
Korea	Hankuk
Lebanon	République Libanaise; Liban
Madagascar (Malagasy Republic)	République Malgache
Mauritania, Islamic Republic of	République Islamique de Mauritanie
Mexico	Estados Unidos Mexicanos
Morocco	Maroc, Royaume de
Mozambique	Moçambique

Netherlands, The	Koninkriyk Der Nederlanden
Netherland Antilles	De Netherlandsche Antillen
Netherlands New Guinea (West Irian)	Nederlands Nieuw Guinea
New Caledonia	Nouvelle Calédonie
New Hebrides	Nouvelles Hébrides
Norway	Norge
Persia	Iran
The Philippines	Repúblika ng Pilipinas
Poland	Polska
Portugal	Republica Portuguesa
Portuguese Guinea	Guiné Portuguesa
Roumania	Republica Populara Romana
Saudi Arabia	Al Mamlaka al Aribiya as-Saudiya
Siam	Thailand
South Africa, Republic of	Suid-Afrika, Republik van
South-West Africa	Suidwes-Afrika
Spain	España
Spanish Guinea	Guinea Española
Spanish Sahara	Sahara Español
Spanish West Africa	Africa Occidental Española
Surinam	Suriname
Sweden	Sverige
Switzerland	Schweiz; Suisse; Svizzera; Helvetia
Tunisia	République Tunisienne
Turkey	Türkiye Cümhuriyeti
Union of Soviet Socialist Republics (U.S.S.R.)	Soyuz Sovetskikh Sotsialisticheskikh Respublik (C.C.C.P.)
Upper Volta (Republic of)	Haute-Volta, République de
Vatican City State	Stato della Citta del Vaticano
Yugoslavia	Federativna Narodna Republika Jugoslavije

10

SIGNATURES OF BISHOPS

IF YOU receive a letter signed, say, *Gerald Cestr*, it will not be from someone with an unusual surname, but from the Bishop of Chester. It is the practice of Church of England bishops to sign their letters with their Christian name (or initials) followed by the name of their episcopal See; and in the case of the older bishoprics the custom is to use a contracted form of the old Latin name of the city or town. The modern name is used where the bishopric is of more recent creation.

In the following list of Anglican bishops in England, the older, contracted Latin forms are followed by a colon (:). Bishops usually add a cross before or after their signatures. The Christian names used are not necessarily those of the present bishops.

Archbishop of Canterbury	Geoffrey Cantuar:
York	Michael Ebor:
Bishop of Bath and Wells	John Bath: et Well:
Birmingham	William Birmingham
Blackburn	Walter Blackburn
Bradford	Donald Bradford
Bristol	Oliver Bristol
Carlisle	Thomas Carliol:
Chelmsford	Frank Chelmsford
Chester	Gerald Cestr:
Chichester	Roger Cicestr:
Coventry	Cuthbert Coventry
Derby	Archibald Derby
Durham	Maurice Dunelm:
Ely	Noel Elien:
Exeter	Robert Exon:
Gloucester	Wilfred Gloucestr:
Guildford	Ivor Guildford
Hereford	Richard Hereford
Leicester	Ronald Leicester
Lichfield	Stanley Lichfield
Lincoln	Kenneth Lincoln:

Liverpool	James Liverpool
London	Henry Londin:
Manchester	Graham Manchester
Newcastle	Hugh Newcastle
Norwich	Percy Norvic:
Oxford	Herbert Oxon:
Peterborough	Ralph Petriburg:
Portsmouth	Leslie Portsmouth
Ripon	George Ripon
Rochester	Charles Roffen:
St Albans	David St Albans
St Edmunds-bury and Ipswich	Harold St Edm. and Ipswich
Salisbury	Gordon Sarum:
Sheffield	Norman Sheffield
Sodor and Man	Benjamin Sodor and Man
Southwark	Bertram Southwark
Southwell	Edmund Southwell
Truro	Frederick Truron:
Wakefield	Joseph Wakefield
Winchester	Alan Winton:
Worcester	Mervyn Worcester

A bishop is not *addressed* by the signature listed above. The form of address for an Anglican bishop is given on page 75.

THE CHURCH OF WALES

Archbishop of Wales	Arthur Cambrensis
Bishop of Bangor	Glyn Bangor
Llandaff	Thomas Landar:
Monmouth	George Monmouth
St Asaph	Alan St Asaph
St David's	David St David's
Swansea and Brecon	Stephen Swansea and Brecon

When a diocesan bishop is elected Archbishop he retains his episcopal see and residence, but uses the signature stated above for Archbishop instead of his signature as a bishop.

EQUIVALENT RANKS IN HM FORCES

ROYAL NAVY	ARMY	ROYAL AIR FORCE
(1) Admiral of the Fleet	Field Marshal	Marshal of the RAF
(2) Admiral	General	Air Chief Marshal
(3) Vice-Admiral	Lieutenant-General	Air Marshal
(4) Rear-Admiral	Major-General	Air Vice-Marshal
(5) Commodore	Brigadier	Air Commodore
(6) Captain	Colonel	Group Captain
(7) Commander	Lieutenant-Colonel	Wing Commander
(8) Lieutenant-Commander	Major	Squadron Leader
(9) Lieutenant	Captain	Flight-Lieutenant
(10) Sub-Lieutenant	Lieutenant	Flying Officer
(11) Senior Commissioned Gunner, &c	Second Lieutenant	Pilot Officer

WOMEN'S SERVICES

In the Women's Royal Army Corps (WRAC) the same ranks are used as for officers in the Army. The Director of the WRAC holds the rank of Brigadier. In the two other services the relative ranks and the titles used are as follows (the numbers correspond with the men's ranks as numbered above):

WOMEN'S ROYAL NAVAL SERVICE (WRNS)	WOMEN'S ROYAL AIR FORCE (WRAF)
(5) Commandant	Air Commandant
(6) Superintendent	Group Officer
(7) Chief Officer	Wing Officer
(8) First Officer	Squadron Officer
(9) Second Officer	Flight Officer
(10) Third Officer	Flying Officer
(11) —	Pilot Officer

ROYAL MARINES

Commissioned officers of the Royal Marines have Army titles of rank. When serving on shore they rank with Army officers of the same titles. When serving afloat a Major, RM, ranks with a Commander, RN; a Captain, RM, with twelve years' service ranks with a Lieutenant-Commander, RN; a Lieutenant, RM, with four years' service ranks with a Lieutenant, RN.

12

PRECEDENCE

Perhaps you have been required to issue invitations to a formal dinner or other social function, and then you are asked to advise on how to seat the guests in their correct order of precedence. Naturally, the Sovereign, or a member of the Royal Family, would be given the chief place; and the president or chairman of the organisation providing the entertainment would take the seat next to the left.

In the absence of Royalty the chief place would be occupied by the Sovereign's representative: Her Majesty's Lieutenant of the county (commonly called the Lord Lieutenant), or the Lord Mayor, or Mayor. The Lieutenant, in his own county, takes precedence over the Lord Mayor or Mayor, even within the latter's own city or borough. But without the Lieutenant, the Lord Mayor or the Mayor, on all municipal occasions, should preside, or act as host, or occupy the chief place.

The official tables of precedence accord the highest rank in the kingdom, after the Royal Family, to the Archbishop of Canterbury, after whom come, in order: the Lord (High) Chancellor, the Archbishop of York, the Prime Minister, the Lord President of the (Privy) Council, the Speaker of the House of Commons, and the Lord Privy Seal. Next in rank are the Ambassadors of foreign countries, and the High Commissioners of the Commonwealth countries. Full tables of precedence are published in the various books of reference on the peerage, *Whitaker's Almanack*, etc.

Precedence among ladies, except Peeresses in their own Right (see page 64), depends on the precedence they derive from their fathers or husbands, if any. A dowager peeress or a baronet's widow (if not remarried) ranks before the peer's or baronet's wife.

Wives and daughters of archbishops and bishops, lieutenants of counties, lord mayors and lord provosts, high sheriffs and sheriffs, mayors and provosts have no special rank or precedence as such. If a peer's daughter marries a peer she takes her husband's rank. If she marries a peer's son she ranks either according to her own precedence as her father's daughter or according to her husband's rank, whichever is higher.

Foreign titles conferred on or inherited by British subjects confer on them no rank or precedence at all in the United Kingdom. They should not be used unless a Royal Licence has been granted. Foreign subjects who inherit British titles may use them, but are not summoned to attend the House of Lords unless they have become British subjects by naturalisation.

13

USEFUL REFERENCE BOOKS

Following are some of the Reference Books that should be available in offices or for consultation in a public library:

Any good Dictionary of the English language.

A good world atlas and gazetteer; and larger scale atlas and gazetteer of the United Kingdom.

Specialised directories and year books appropriate to specific interests of the office; and telephone directories.

FOR GENERAL INFORMATION:

Encyclopaedia Britannica
Chambers's Encyclopaedia

Whitaker's Almanack
Pears Cyclopaedia

Keesing's Contemporary Archives (which build up through the year)

FOR SPECIAL INFORMATION:

Annual Register of World Events
British Books in Print
Brit. Commonwealth & International Trades Index
Burke's Peerage
Crockford's Clerical Directory
Commonwealth Universities YB
Debrett's Peerage
Directory of Directors
Dod's Parliamentary Companion
Guinness Book of Records
International Who's Who
Kelly's Handbook of Titled, Landed & Official Classes

Kelly's Post Office London Directory
Law List
Municipal YB
Newspaper Press Directory
Post Office Guide
Scottish Law List
Statesman's YB
Stock Exchange Official YB
Technical Books in Print
Titles & Forms of Address
Who's Who
Writers' & Artists' YB

ABBREVIATIONS OF ENGLISH AND WELSH COUNTIES

THE FOLLOWING abbreviations of the names of counties in England and Wales are acceptable for use on letters:

Beds.	for Bedfordshire	Mon.	for	Monmouthshire
Berks.	Berkshire	Northants.		Northamptonshire
Bucks.	Buckinghamshire	Notts.		Nottinghamshire
Cambs.	Cambridgeshire	Oxon.		Oxfordshire
Carms.	Carmarthenshire	Pembs.		Pembrokeshire
Glam.	Glamorgan	Salop.		Shropshire
Glos.	Gloucestershire	Staffs.		Staffordshire
Hants.	Hampshire	Sx		Sussex
Herts.	Hertfordshire	Wilts.		Wiltshire
Lancs.	Lancashire	Worcs.		Worcestershire
Lincs.	Lincolnshire	Yorks.		Yorkshire
Middx	Middlesex			

COUNTY TOWNS

Following are the towns containing the administrative headquarters of each **ENGLISH** county:

Beds.:	Bedford	Herts.:	Hertford
Berks.:	Reading	Hunts. &	
Bucks.:	Aylesbury	Peterboro':	Huntingdon
Cambs. & Ely:	Cambridge	Kent:	Maidstone
Cheshire:	Chester	Lancs.:	Preston
Cornwall:	Truro	Lincs.—	
Cumberl'd:	Carlisle	Holland:	Boston
Derbyshire:	Matlock	Kesteven:	Sleaford
Devon:	Exeter	Lindsey:	Lincoln
Dorset:	Dorchester	Norfolk:	Norwich
Durham:	Durham	Northants.:	Northampton
Essex:	Chelmsford	Northumb'ld:	Newcastle on
Glos.:	Gloucester		Tyne
Hants.:	Winchester	Notts.:	Nottingham
Herefordshire:	Hereford	Oxon.:	Oxford

Rutland:	Oakham	W. Sussex:	Chichester
Shropshire:	Shrewsbury	Warwickshire:	Warwick
Somerset:	Taunton	Westmorland:	Kendal
Staffs.:	Stafford	Wight, Isle of:	Newport
E. Suffolk:	Ipswich	Wilts.:	Trowbridge
W. Suffolk:	Bury St Edmunds	Worcs.:	Worcester
		Yorks. (York)—	
Surrey:	Kingston on Thames	E. Riding:	Beverley
		N. Riding:	Northallerton
E. Sussex:	Lewes	W. Riding:	Wakefield

Following are the towns containing the administrative headquarters of each **WELSH** county:

Anglesey	Llangefni	Glamorgan	Cardiff
Brecknockshire or Breconshire	Brecon	Merioneth	Dolgellau
		Monmouthshire	Newport
Caernarvonshire	Caernarvon	Montgomeryshire	Welshpool
Cardiganshire	Aberystwyth	Pembrokeshire	Haverfordwest
Carmarthenshire	Carmarthen	Radnorshire	Llandrindod Wells
Denbighshire	Ruthin		
Flintshire	Mold		

Following are the towns containing the administrative headquarters of each **SCOTTISH** county:

Aberdeen	Aberdeen	Lanarkshire	Hamilton
Angus	Forfar	Midlothian	Edinburgh
Argyll	Lochgilphead	Morayshire	Elgin
Ayrshire	Ayr	Nairn	Nairn
Banffshire	Banff	Orkney	Kirkwall
Berwickshire	Duns	Peeblesshire	Peebles
Bute	Rothesay	Perthshire	Perth
Caithness	Wick	Renfrewshire	Paisley
Clackmannan	Alloa	Ross & Cromarty	Dingwall
Dumfriesshire	Dumfries		
Dunbartonshire	Dumbarton	Roxburghshire	Newton St Boswells
East Lothian	Haddington		
Fife	Cupar	Selkirkshire	Selkirk
Inverness-shire	Inverness	Stirlingshire	Stirling
Kincardineshire	Stonehaven	Sutherland	Golspie
		West Lothian	Linlithgow
Kinross-shire	Kinross	Wigtownshire	Stranraer
Kirkcudbrightshire	Kirkcudbright	Zetland	Lerwick

ABBREVIATIONS OF THE UNITED STATES

THE FOLLOWING are the fifty States (and the Federal District of Columbia) of the United States of America, with recognised abbreviations:

Alabama	Ala.	Montana	Mont.
Alaska		Nebraska	Nebr.
Arizona	Ariz.	Nevada	Nev.
Arkansas	Ark.	New Hampshire	N.H.
California	Cal.	New Jersey	N.J.
Colorado	Colo.	New Mexico	N.Mex.
Connecticut	Conn.	New York	N.Y.
Delaware	Del.	North Carolina	N.C.
Dist. of Columbia	D.C.	North Dakota	N.Dak.
Florida	Fla.	Ohio	O.
Georgia	Ga.	Oklahoma	Okla.
Hawaii		Oregon	Oreg.
Idaho		Pennsylvania	Pa.
Illinois	Ill.	Rhode Island	R.I.
Indiana	Ind.	South Carolina	S.C.
Iowa		South Dakota	S.Dak.
Kansas	Kan.	Tennessee	Tenn.
Kentucky	Ky.	Texas	Tex.
Louisiana	La.	Utah	
Maine	Me.	Vermont	Vt.
Maryland	Md.	Virginia	Va.
Massachusetts	Mass.	Washington	Wash.
Michigan	Mich.	West Virginia	W.Va.
Minnesota	Minn.	Wisconsin	Wis.
Mississippi	Miss.	Wyoming	Wy.
Missouri	Mo.		

CANADIAN ABBREVIATIONS

The following are the ten Provinces of the Dominion of Canada, with recognised abbreviations:

Alberta	Alta.	Ontario	Ont.
British Columbia	B.C.	Prince Edward	
Manitoba	Man.	Island	P.E.I.
New Brunswick	N.B.	Quebec	P.Q.
Newfoundland	Nfld.	Saskatchewan	Sask.
Nova Scotia	N.S.		

GENERAL ABBREVIATIONS

ABBREVIATIONS ARE shortened forms of words, or the initial letters of some or all of the words, that form a title, the name of an organisation, a form of address of a person, or a proverb or form of reference.

Many of the groups of capital letters which may be placed after the name or title of persons entitled to them begin with a letter (or letters) representing one of the following: Associate, Associate Member, Bachelor, Companion, Doctor, Fellow, Licentiate, Master, or Member; or the word Royal. These are grouped together in these pages for convenience, but therefore may appear slightly out of alphabetical order.

Some abbreviations consist of capital letters, or capital and small letters: others are generally written with small letters only, unless they begin a sentence. Fullstops are omitted from the capital-letter abbreviations: their use after each letter is entirely optional. With abbreviations in small letters, stops should be used as given in these pages.

Abbreviations are sometimes initials or parts of Latin or foreign words. These words are given in brackets, followed by the English words for which they are used.

For abbreviations of counties, American States and Canadian Provinces see previous pages.

A

A	Academy; America; Associate; anna
a	acre; alto; adjective; anna (coin)
AA	Automobile Association; Anti-aircraft
AAA	Amateur Athletic Association
A and M	Hymns Ancient and Modern
AAG	Assistant Adjutant General
AB	able-bodied seaman; (Aktiebolaget) Swedish equivalent of Eng. 'Ltd'.
ABA	Amateur Boxing Association
abbr	abbreviation; abbreviated
ABC	alphabet; Aerated Bread Company; a railway guide so named
ab init.	(*ab initio*) from the beginning
Abl	ablative
Abp	Archbishop
abr	abridged; abridgment

AC	(*ante Christum*) Before the birth of Christ; Air-craftman; Aero Club; Alpine Club
ac	alternating current; author's correction
a/c (or acct)	account
Acad	Academy
ACC	Assistant County Commissioner; Army Catering Corps; Assistant Chief Constable
Acc	accusative; acceptance
acc	acceded
accel	(*accelerando*) with increasing speed (*music*)
ACF	Army Cadet Force
ACG	Assistant Chaplain General
ACIGS	Assistant Chief, Imperial General Staff
ACM	Air Chief Marshal
AD	(*Anno Domini*) In the year of our Lord
ad	advertisement
a.d.	(*ante diem*) before the day; after date
ADC	Aide-de-camp; Army Dental Corps; Assistant District Commissioner
ADGB	Air Defence of Great Britain
ad inf	(*ad infinitum*) to infinity, without limit
ad int	(*ad interim*) in the meantime
Adj	Adjutant; adjective
ad lib	(*ad libitum*) at pleasure, as you please
ADM	Annual Delegate Meeting
Adm	Admiral
Admin	Administration; administrative
ADMS	Assistant Director of Medical Services
ADOS	Assistant Director of Ordnance Services
Adv	adverb
ad val	(*ad valorem*) according to the value
ADVS	Assistant Director of Veterinary Services
Advt	Advertisement
AEA	Air Efficiency Award; Atomic Energy Authority
AEC	Atomic Energy Commission
AEF	Amalgamated Union of Engineering and Foundry Workers
AERE	Atomic Energy Research Establishment
aet (or aetat)	(*aetatis*) aged, of age, so many years
AEU	Amalgamated Engineering Union
AF	Admiral of the Fleet; Army Form
AFA	Amateur Football (or Fencing) Association
AFC	Air Force Cross; Amateur Football Club
afft	affidavit
AFM	Air Force Medal
AFS	Auxiliary Fire Service; Atlantic Ferry Service

AG	Adjutant (Attorney; Accountant; Agent) General; (*Aktiengesellschaft*) German equivalent of Eng. 'Ltd'.
Ag	(*argentum*) silver
AGM	Annual General Meeting
AH	(*Anno Hegirae*) In the year of Hegira (AD 622)
AIAA	Architect Member, Incorporated Association of Architects and Surveyors
AID	Aeronautical Inspection Department (Ministry of Technology); Army Intelligence Department; Artificial Insemination Donor
AL	(*Anno Lucis*) In the year of Light
alt	altitude
AM	(*Anno Mundi*) In the year of the World; Albert Medal; Air Marshal; Master of Arts
am	(*ante meridiem*) before noon; in the morning
AMA	Assistant Masters' Association
AMD	Army Medical Department
AMDG	(*Ad majorem Dei Gloriam*) To the greater glory of God
Amt	Amount
Anal	Analogy; analogous
Anat	Anatomy
Anon	Anonymous; anonymously
ANZAC	Australian and New Zealand Army Corps
AOA	Air Officer, Administration
AOC	Air Officer Commanding
AOC-in-C	Air Officer Commanding-in-Chief
AOD	Army Ordnance Department; Ancient Order of Druids
AOF	Ancient Order of Foresters
AOH	Ancient Order of Hibernians
ap	above proof (spirits); author's proof (printing)
APD	Army Pay Department
APMG	Assistant Postmaster General
approx	approximately
APTC	Army Physical Training Corps
AQMG	Assistant Quartermaster-General
ARCE	Academical Rank of Civil Engineers
arch	archipelago; archaism; archaic
Archd	Archdeacon
Archit	Architect; architectural
ARP	Air Raid Precautions (Service)
Art	Artist; artillery; article; artificial
AS	Anglo-Saxon; Account Sales; Academy of Science

ASA	Amateur Swimming Association
ASDIC	Anti-Submarine Detector Indicator Committee

*   *   *

ASSOCIATES	ASSOCIATE (OF THE)
AACCA	Association of Certified and Corporate Accountants
AAI	Chartered Auctioneers and Estate Agents' Institute
AAIA	Association of International Accountants
AASA	Australian Society of Accounts
ABI (or ACBI)	Institute of Book-keepers
ACA	Institute of Chartered Accountants in England and Wales
ACCS	Corporation of Certified Secretaries
ACGI	City and Guilds (of London) Institute
ACIA	Corporation of Insurance Agents
ACIB	Corporation of Insurance Brokers
ACIS	Chartered Institute of Secretaries
ACommA	Society of Commercial Accountants
ACP	College of Preceptors
AERA	Engraver, Royal Academy
AFA	Faculty of Actuaries
AFAS	Faculty of Architects and Surveyors
AFRAeS	Fellow of Royal Aeronautical Society
AGI	Institute of Certified Grocers
AGSM	Guildhall School of Music
AIA	Institute of Actuaries
AIAC	Institute of Company Accountants
AIAE	Institute of Automobile Engineers
AIArb	Institute of Arbitrators
AIAS	Incorporated Association of Architects and Surveyors
AIB	Institute of Bankers
AIBD	Institute of British Decorators
AIC	Institute of Chemistry
AICS	Institute of Chartered Shipbrokers
AIFireE	Institute of Fire Engineers
AIHA	Institute of Hospital Almoners
AIHVE	Institute of Heating and Ventilating Engineers
AIIA	Institute of Industrial Administration
AIM	Institute of Metallurgists
AIMarE	Institute of Marine Engineers
AIMechE	Institution of Mechanical Engineers
AIMinE	Institute of Mining Engineers
AIMSW	Institute of Medical Social Workers (Almoners)

AIMTA	Institute of Municipal Treasurers and Accountants
AINA	Institution of Naval Architects
A InstAA	Institute of Automobile Assessors
A Inst MSM	Institute of Marketing and Sales Management
AIOB	Institute of Builders
AIS	Institute of Statisticians
AIStruct E	Institute of Structural Engineers
AIQS	Institute of Quantity Surveyors
AKC	King's College, London
ALA	Library Association
ALAA	London Association of Certified Accountants
ALCD	London College of Divinity
ALCM	London College of Music
ALS	Linnaean Society
AMA	Museums Association
ANA	National Academician (USA)
APS	Pharmaceutical Society
ARA	Royal Academy
ARAD	Royal Academy of Dancing
ARAeS	Royal Aeronautical Society
ARAM	Royal Academy of Music
ARBA	Royal Society of British Artists
ARBC	Royal British Colonial Society of Artists
ARCA	Royal College of Art; Royal Cambrian Academy
ARCI	Royal Colonial Institute
ARCM	Royal College of Music
ARCO	Royal College of Organists
ARCS	Royal College of Science
ARE	Royal Society of Painter Etchers
ARHA	Royal Hibernian Academy
ARIBA	Royal Institute of British Architects
ARIC	Royal Institute of Chemistry
ARICS	Royal Institute of Chartered Surveyors
ARMS	Royal Society of Miniature Painters
ARPS	Royal Photographic Society
ARRC	Royal Red Cross (order)
ARSanI	Royal Sanitary Institute
ARSL	Royal Society of Literature
ARSM	Royal School of Mines
ARVA	Incorporated Association of Rating and Valuation Auditors
ARWS	Royal Society of Painters in Water Colours
ASAA	Society of Incorporated Accountants and Auditors

ASAM	Society of Art Masters
ATCL	Trinity College of Music, London
ATS	Theological Study
AVA	Valuers' Association

*   *   *

ASSOCIATED MEMBER OF

AMBIM	British Institute of Management
AMIAE	Institute of Automobile Engineers
AMIAMA	Incorporated Advertising Managers Association
AMIBiol	Institute of Biology
AMICE	Institution of Civil Engineers
AMIChem E	Institution of Chemical Engineers
AMICM	Institute of Credit Management
AMIEE	Institution of Electrical Engineers
AMIFire E	Institute of Fire Engineers
AMIGas E	Institute of Gas Engineers
AMIIA	Institute of Industrial Administrators
AMILoco E	Institute of Locomotive Engineers
AMIMar E	Institute of Marine Engineers
AMIMech E	Institution of Mechanical Engineers
AMI Min E	Institution of Mining Engineers
AMINA	Institutional Management Association
AMInst TE	Institution of Transport Engineers
AMIPA	Institute of Practitioners in Advertising
AMIPHE	Institution of Public Health Engineers
AMIStruct E	Institution of Structural Engineers
AMIWM	Institution of Works Managers
AMRINA	Royal Institution of Naval Architects

*   *   *

ASE	Amalgamated Society of Engineers
ASGB	Aeronautical Society of Great Britain
ASLEF	Associated Society of Locomotive Engineers and Firemen
ASLIB	Association of Special Libraries and Information Bureaux
ASM	Assistant Stage Manager
Assn or Assoc	Association
Asst	Assistant
ATA	Air Transport Auxiliary
ATC	Air Training Corps; Art Teachers' Certificate
ATD	Art Teacher's Diploma
ATS	Auxiliary Territorial Service
att	attached
Atty Gen	Attorney General
Auxil	Auxiliary

AV	Authorised Version
AVD	Army Veterinary Department
avdp	avoirdupois (weight)
AVM	Air Vice-Marshal
AWOL	Absent without official leave

B

B	Baron; Bachelor; black (of pencils)
b	born; brother; bowled (cricket)
BA	British Academy

* * *

BACHELORS	BACHELOR OF
BA	Arts
BAO	Obstetrics
BArch	Architecture
BCE	Civil Engineering
BCh (or BChir)	Surgery
BCL	Civil Law
BComm	Commerce
BD	Divinity
BDS (or BChD)	Dental Surgery
BEd	Education
BEng	Engineering
BL	Law
BLitt	Letters; Literature
BLL (or LLB)	Laws
BM	Medicine
BMet	Metallurgy
BME	Mining Engineering
BMus	Music
BPharm	Pharmacy
BPhil	Philosophy
BS	Surgery
BSc	Science
BScTech	Technical Science
BTech	Technology
BUJ	Canon and Civil Law
BVMS	Veterinary Medicine and Surgery

* * *

Bal	Balance
BAOR	British Army of the Rhine
BALPA	British Airline Pilots Association
Bapt	Baptist; baptised
Bar	Barrister-at-law
Bart (or Bt)	Baronet
BB	Boys' Brigade; double black (of pencils)

BBC	British Broadcasting Corporation
BC	Before Christ
BCF	British Cycling Federation
BDA	British Dental Association
BEA	British European Airways; British Esperanto Assoc.
Bdr	Bombardier
BDS	Bomb Disposal Squad
BEF	British Expeditionary Force
BEM	British Empire Medal
BENA	British Empire Naturalists Association
BESA	British Engineering Standards Association
BETAA	British Export Trade Advertising Association
BETRO	British Export Trade Research Organisation
b/fwd	brought forward
BGGS	Brigadier General, General Staff
BIF	British Industries Fair
BIM	British Institute of Marketing
BISF	British Iron and Steel Federation
BL	Barrister-at-Law; Bachelor of Law
B/L	Bill of Lading
BLESMA	British Limbless Ex-Servicemen's Association
BMA	British Medical Association
BNC	Brasenose College (Oxford)
BOT	Board of Trade
Bot	Botany; botanical
BOU	British Ornithologists' Union
Bp	Bishop; below proof; boiling point
BQ	(*Bene quiescat*) may he (or she) repose well
BQMS	Battery Quartermaster-Sergeant
BR	British Railways (or Rail)
BRCS	British Red Cross Society
Brig	Brigade; Brigadier
BRS	British Road Services
BSA	Boy Scouts Association
BSI	British Standards Institute
BST	British Summer Time; British Standard Time
Bt	Baronet
Btu (*or* B Th U)	British Thermal Unit
Bur	Buried
BVM	Blessed Virgin Mary

C

C	Chancellor; Centigrade; Conservative; Church; Catholic; (*centum*) 100; Cape; common metre (music)

c	caught (cricket); circa (about); chapter; cubic; cent
CA	County Alderman; Church Army; Chartered Accountant
CA Att	Civil Air Attaché
CAB	Citizens' Advice Bureau
CAEC	County Agricultural Executive Committee
c&b	caught and bowled (by same man) (cricket)
Can	Canada; canton; canto; cantoris
Cantab (or Camb)	(Cantabrigia) Cambridge
Cant	Canterbury; Canticles
Cap	Capital letter; chapter; number of an Act of Parliament
Capt	Captain
CAS	Chief of Air Staff
CAT	College of Advanced Technology
CATC	Commonwealth Air Transport Council
Cav	Cavalry
CB	Companion of the Bath; Confined to Barracks; Cavalry Brigade
CBI	Confederation of British Industries
CBE	Commander of the British Empire (Order)
CBS	Columbia Broadcasting System
CBSA	Clay Bird Shooting Association
CC	County Councillor; County Council; Cricket Club; County Commissioner; City Council
cc	cubic centimetre(s)
CCF	Combined Cadet Force
CD	Civil Defence; Corps Diplomatique (Diplomatic Corps)
Cdr	Commander
CE	Civil Engineer: Common Era; Chief Engineer
CEGB	Central Electricity Generating Board
cent	(centum) a hundred; century
CENTO	Central Treaty Organisation (Baghdad Pact)
CERN	European Centre for Nuclear Research
CETS	Church of England Temperance Society
CF	Chaplain of the Forces
cf	(confer) compare; calf; carry forward
CG	Coldstream Guards; Captain-General; Consul-General
CGM	Conspicuous Gallantry Medal
CGS	Centimetre–gramme–second (system); Chief of the General Staff
CH	Companion of Honour; clearing house
Ch	Church

Chap	chapter
ChB	Bachelor of Surgery
ChCh	Christ Church, Oxford
Chem	Chemistry; chemical
ChM	Master of Surgery
CI	Lady of the Order of the Crown of India; Channel Islands
CID	Criminal Investigation Department; Council of Industrial Design
CIE	Companion of the Indian Empire (Order)
cif	cost, insurance, and freight
CIGS	Chief of Imperial General Staff
C-in-C	Commander-in-Chief
CI Mech E	Companion of the Institution of Mechanical Engineers
CIO	Congress of Industrial Organisations (USA); Central (or Church of England) Information Office
CIV	City Imperial Volunteers
Civ	Civil; civilian
CJ	Chief Justice
CLB	Central Land Board; Church Lads' Brigade
CM	Master of Surgery; Certified Master
cm	centimetre
Cmd	Command
Cmd'd	Commanded
Cmdg	Commanding
Cmdr	Commander
Cmdre	Commodore
Cmdt	Commandant
CMF	Central Mediterranean Force
CMG	Companion of St Michael and St George (Order)
CMS	Church Missionary Society
Cmsr	Commissioner
CNAA	Council for National Academic Awards
CND	Campaign for Nuclear Disarmament
CO	Commanding Officer; Colonial (or Crown) Office; Conscientious Objector
Co	Company; County
c/o	in care of; carried over
Coad	Coadjutor
COD	Cash on Delivery
C of E	Church of England
COI	Central Office of Information
Col	Column; Colonel

Coll	College
Com	Committee
COMECON	Council for Mutual Economic Assistance
Con	(*contra*) in opposition; Consul
Con esp	(*con espressione*) with expression (music)
Conj	Conjugation
COO	Chief Ordnance Officer
COS	Charity Organisation Society; Chief of Staff
cos	cosine (mathematics)
CP	Common Pleas; Clerk of the Peace; Code of Procedure
cp	compare; carriage paid
CPA	Certified Public Accountant
Cpl	Corporal
CPO	Chief Petty Officer
CPRE	Council for the Preservation of Rural England
CQMS	Company Quartermaster-Sergeant
CR	Community of the Resurrection
cr	credit; creditor; created; creation (peerage)
CRA	Commanding (or Commander of) Royal Artillery
CRE	Commanding (or Commander of) Royal Engineers
cres	(*crescendo*) increasingly loud (*music*)
CRT	Cathode-ray tube
CS	Civil Service; Court of Session
CSC	Civil Service Commission; Conspicuous Service Cross
CSE	Certificate of Secondary Education
CSI	Companion of the Star of India (Order); Chartered Surveyors' Institution
CSM	Company Sergeant Major
CSSR	Congregation of Most Holy Redeemer (Redemptorists)
CT	College of Technology
CTC	Cyclists Touring Club
CU	Cambridge University
CV	Common Version (Bible)
CVO	Commander of the Royal Victorian Order
cwo	cash with order
CWS	Co-operative Wholesale Society
cwt	hundredweight

D

D	Duke
d	(*denarius*) penny; died; daughter

D & C	Dilation and Curettage
D & D	Drunk and Disorderly
DA	Diploma in Anaesthetics
DAAG	Deputy Assistant Adjutant General
DACG	Deputy Assistant Chaplain General
DADMS	Deputy Assistant Director Medical Services
DADOS	Deputy Assistant Director Ordnance Services
DADQ	Deputy Assistant Director of Quartering
DAG	Deputy Adjutant-General; Development Assistance Group
DAPM	Deputy Assistant Provost-Marshal
DAQMG	Deputy Assistant Quartermaster-General
DAR	Daughters of the American Revolution
DAS	Dramatic Authors' Society
Dat	Dative
DATA	Draughtsmen and Allied Technicians Assoc.
Dau	Daughter
DB	Domesday Book
db	Decibel
DBE	Dame Commander of British Empire (Order)
DC	District of Columbia; District Commissioner; (*da capo*) from the beginning; again (*music*)
dc	direct current
DCAe	Diploma of College of Aeronautics
DCLI	Duke of Cornwall's Light Infantry
DCM	Distinguished Conduct Medal
DCMG	Dame Commander of St Michael and St George (Order)
DCVO	Dame Commander of Royal Victorian Order
DDMS	Deputy Director of Medical Services
DDOS	Deputy Director Ordnance Services
DDT	Dichloro-Diphenyl-Trichloroethane (insecticide)
DEA	Department of Economic Affairs
Deb	Debutante; debenture
dec	decimal; deceased
deg	degree
del	(*delineavit*) he (or she) drew it
dep	departs (train); deputy
dept	department
decres	(*decrescendo*) same as dim. (q.v.)
DEP	Department of Employment and Productivity
DEW	Distant Early Warning (defence line)
DF	Dean of Faculty; Defender of the Faith
DFC	Distinguished Flying Cross
DFM	Distinguished Flying Medal

DG	(*Dei gratia*) By the Grace of God; Director-General; Dragoon Guards
DGMS	Director General of Medical Services
DGMW	Director General of Military Works
Dial	Dialect
DIC	Diploma of the Imperial College
Dim	diminutive
dim	(*diminuendo*) decrease the sound (*music*)
Dip Inst MSM	Diploma in Marketing, Institute of Marketing and Sales Management
dist	district; distant
DL	Deputy-Lieutenant
DLI	Durham Light Infantry
DM	Deputy Master; Doctor of Medicine
dm	(*destra mano*) with the right hand (music)
DMI	Director of Military Intelligence
DMRE	Diploma in Medical Radiology and Electrology
DMS	Director of Medical Services
DNB	Dictionary of National Biography
DNI	Director of Naval Intelligence
DO	Diploma in Ophthalmology

*   *   *

DOCTORS	DOCTOR OF
DCh	Surgery
DCL	Civil Law
DCnL	Canon Law
DCT	Christian Theology
DD	Divinity
DDS	Dental Surgery
DDSc	Dental Science
DEng	Engineering
DHL	Hebrew Literature
D Lit; Litt D	Literature; Letters
D Litt	Letters (Aberdeen)
D Hy	Hygiene
DLC	Celtic Literature
DLS	Library Science
DM	Medicine (Oxford)
DMus	Music
DPh; PhD	Philosophy
D Soc Sc	Social Sciences
D Sc	Science
D Th	Theology
DVSc	Veterinary Science (or Surgery)
DZ	Zoology

*   *   *   *

DOM	(*Dominus Omnium Magister*) God (is) Master of All
DORA	Defence of the Realm Act
D Opt	Diploma in Ophthalmics of Institute of Optical Science
DOS	Director of Ordnance Services (or Survey)
doz	dozen
DP	Displaced Persons; Drill Purposes
DPAS	Discharged Prisoners Aid Society
DPH	Diploma in Public Health
DPM	Diploma in Psychological Medicine; Deputy Provost-Marshal
dr	doctor; debtor
DRCOG	Diploma of Royal College of Obstetricians and Gynaecologists
DSC	Distinguished Service Cross
DSM	Distinguished Service Medal
DSO	Distinguished Service Order (Companion of)
dsp	(*decessit sine prole*) died without issue
dspl	(*decessit sine prole legitima*) died without legitimate issue
dspm	(*decessit sine prole mascula*) died without male issue
dspms	(*decessit sine prole mascula supersite*) died without surviving male issue
dsps	(*decessit sine prole superstite*) died without surviving issue
DSSc	Diploma in Sanitary Science
DTD	Decoration for Devoted Service (South Africa)
DTM	Diploma in Tropical Medicine
d unm	died unmarried
DV	(*Deo volente*) God willing
dvm	(*decessit vita matris*) died in lifetime of mother
dvp	(*decessit vita patris*) died in lifetime of father
dwt	pennyweight

E

E	East; Earl; Earth; Eastern
E and OE	Errors and Omissions Excepted
EB	Encyclopaedia Britannica
Ebor	(Eboracum) York
E b S	East-by-South
EC	East Central (District); Episcopalian Church; Executive Committee
ECA	Economic Commission for Africa
eccles	ecclesiastical

ECSC	European Coal and Steel Community
ED	Efficiency Decoration
EdB	Bachelor of Education
Ed	Editor; edition; educated
EE	Errors Excepted
EEC	European Economic Community (Common Market)
EETS	Early English Text Society
EFTA	European Free Trade Association
eg	(*exempli gratia*) for example
EGM	Empire Gallantry Medal
EICS	East India Company's Service
El	Eldest
ELCr	Engineer Lieutenant-Commander (Naval)
EM	Earl Marshal; Edward Medal
EMA	European Monetary Agreement
ENE	East-North-East
Eng	England; English; engineer; engineering
ENSA	Entertainments National Service Association
E&OE	Errors and Omissions Excepted
EOM	Egyptian Order of Merit
EP	Extended Play (record)
EPU	European Payments Union
ER	(*Elizabeth Regina*) Queen Elizabeth; (*Edwardus Rex*) King Edward; East Riding of Yorks.
ERD	Emergency Reserve Decoration
ERNIE	Electronic Random Number Indicator Equipment
ERP	European Recovery Plan
ERU	English Rugby Union
ESE	East-South-East
ESP	Extra-Sensory Perception
esp	especially
Esq	Esquire
etc (or &c)	(*et cetera*) and other things
et seq	(*et sequentia*) and the following
ETU	Electrical Trades Union
EURATOM	European Atomic Energy Community
EVA	Engineer Vice-Admiral
Ex	Example; exception; exercise
Exc	Excellency
ex lib	(*ex libris*) from the books of
ex n (or xn)	without the right to new shares
Exor	Executor
Exrx	Executrix
ext	external; extinct; extract

F

F	Fahrenheit; Father; Fellow
f	feet; fathom; franc; furlong; following; (*forte*) loud (*music*)
FA	Football Association
FAA	Fleet Air Arm
Fahr	Fahrenheit
FAM	Free and Accepted Masons
FANY	First Aid Nursing Yeomanry
FAO	Food and Agriculture Organisation (of UN)
FAP	First Aid Post
FAVO	Fleet Aviation Officer
FBI	Federal Bureau of Investigation (USA)
FC	Football Club
fscp	foolscap (size of paper)
FD	(*Fidei Defensor*) Defender of the Faith
fec	(*fecit*) He (or she) did (or made) it
Fedr	Federation

*   *   *

FELLOWS	FELLOW of the
FACCA	Association of Certified and Corporate Accountants
FACS	American College of Surgeons
FADO	Association of Dispensing Opticians
FAGS	American Geographical Society
FAI	Chartered Auctioneers and Estate Agents Institute
FAIA	Association of International Accountants
FAII	Australian Insurance Institute
FALPA	Incorporated Society Auctioneers and Landed Property Agents
FAO	United Nations Food and Agriculture Organisation
FAS	Antiquarian Society; Anthropological Society
FASB	Asiatic Society of Bengal
FBA	British Academy
FBAA	British Association of Accountants and Auditors
FBEA	British Esperanto Association
FBIM	British Institute of Management
FBOA	British Optical Association
FBOU	British Ornithologists Union
FBS	Botanical Society
FCA	Institute of Chartered Accountants
FCCS	Corporation of Certified Secretaries
FCGI	City and Guilds (of London) Institute

FCIA	Corporation of Insurance Agents
FCIB	Corporation of Insurance Brokers
FCII	Chartered Insurance Institute
FCIS	Chartered Institute of Secretaries
FCP	College of Preceptors
FCRA	Corporation of Registered Accountants
FCS	Chemical Society
FCSP	Chartered Society of Physiotherapists
FCST	College of Speech Therapists
FCTB	College of Teachers of the Blind
FCWA	Institute of Cost and Works Accountants
FEIS	Educational Institute of Scotland
FES	Entomological Society; Ethnological Society
FFA	Faculty of Actuaries
FFA,RCS	Faculty of Anaesthetists, Royal College of Surgeons
FFAS	Faculty of Architects and Surveyors
FFI	Faculty of Insurance
FGI	Institute of Certificated Grocers
FGO	Guild of Organists
FGS	Geological Society
FHAS	Highland and Agricultural Society of Scotland
FHS	Heraldry Society
FIA	Institute of Actuaries
FIAA	Incorporated Association of Architects and Surveyors (Architect Member)
FIAC	Institute of Company Accountants
FIAMA	Incorporated Advertising Managers Assoc.
FI Arb	Institute of Arbitrators
FIAS	Incorporated Association of Architects and Surveyors (Surveyor Member)
FIB	Institute of Bankers
FIBD	Institute of British Decorators
FICS	Institute of Chartered Shipbrokers
FID	Institute of Directors
FIF	Institute of Fuel
FIH	Institute of Hygiene
FIIA	Institute of Industrial Administration
FIInst	Imperial Institute
FIMTA	Institute of Municipal Treasurers and Accountants
FIncST	Incorporated Society of Shorthand Teachers
FInstMSM	Institute of Marketing and Sales Management
FInstP	Institute of Physics
FIO	Institute of Ophthalmic Opticians
FIOB	Institute of Building

FIPA	Institute of Practitioners in Advertising
FIPI	Institute of Patentees, Incorporated
FIPR	Institute of Public Relations
FIPS	Institute of Private Secretaries
FIQS	Institute of Quantity Surveyors
FISA	Incorporated Secretaries Association
FISE	Institution of Structural Engineers
FIWM	Institution of Works Managers
FIWT	Institute of Wireless Technology
FJI	Institute of Journalists
FKC; FKCL	King's College, London
FLA	Library Association
FLAA	London Association of Certified Accountants
FLAS	Chartered Land Agents' Society
FLGA	Local Government Association
FLS	Linnaean Society
FMS	Medical Society
FPS	Pharmaceutical Society
FPhS	Philosophical Society of England
FPhyS	Physical Society
FRAeS	Royal Aeronautical Society
FRAI	Royal Anthropological Institute
FRAM	Royal Academy of Music
FRAS	Royal Astronomical Society; Royal Asiatic Society
FRBS	Royal Botanic Society; Royal Society of British Sculptors
FRCI	Royal Colonial Institute
FRCM	Royal College of Music
FRCOG	Royal College of Obstetricians and Gynaecologists
FRCP(Ed) (I)	Royal College of Physicians (Edinburgh) (Ireland)
FRCS	Royal College of Surgeons
FRCVS	Royal College of Veterinary Surgeons
FREcon Soc	Royal Economic Society
FRFPS(G)	Royal Faculty of Physicians and Surgeons, Glasgow
FRGS	Royal Geographical Society
FRHist Soc	Royal Historical Society
FRHS	Royal Horticultural Society
FRI	Royal Institution
FRIAS	Royal Incorporation of Architects in Scotland
FRIBA	Royal Institute of British Architects
FRIC	Royal Institute of Chemistry
FRICS	Royal Institute of Chartered Surveyors

FRMS	Royal Microscopical Society
FRMCS	Royal Medical and Chirurgical Society
FRMetS	Royal Meteorological Society
FRNS	Royal Numismatic Society
FRNSA	Royal School of Naval Architecture
FRPS	Royal Photographic Society
FRPSL	Royal Philatelic Society, London
FRS	Royal Society
FRSA	Royal Society of Arts
FRSAI	Royal Society of Antiquaries, Ireland
FRSan I	Royal Sanitary Institute
FRSC	Royal Society of Canada
FRSE	Royal Society of Edinburgh
FRSGS	Royal Scottish Geographical Society
FRSL	Royal Society of Literature
FRSSA	Royal Scottish Society of Arts
FRSSI (or S)	Royal Statistical Society of Ireland (or Scotland)
FRVA	Incorporated Association of Rating and Valuation Officers
FRZS Scot	Royal Zoological Society of Scotland
FSA	Society of Antiquaries
FSAA	Society of Incorporated Accountants and Auditors
FSAL	Society of Antiquaries of London
FSMC	Spectacle Makers Company
FSS	Statistical Society
FSScA	Society of Science and Art, London
FTCD	Trinity College, Dublin
FTCL	Trinity College (of Music) London
FTI	Textile Institute
FVA	Valuers' Association
FZS	Zoological Society

* * *

FFHC	Freedom from Hunger Campaign
FGCM	Field General Court Martial
FH	Fire hydrant
Fid Def	(*Fidei Defensor*) Defender of the Faith
FIDO	Fog Investigation Dispersal Operation
fig	figure
F/Lt	Flight Lieutenant
FM	Field Marshal
FMS	Federated Malay States
FO	Foreign Office; Field Officer; Flying Officer
fo	(folio) page
ff or fff	(*fortissimo*) very loudly (*music*)

fob	free on board
fol	following
FS	Flight-Sergeant (RAF); Fleet Surgeon
ft	fort; feet
fv	(*folio verso*) on the back of the page

G

G	Gulf
g	acceleration of gravity; guinea
GA	General Assembly
gal	gallon
GATT	General Agreement on Tariffs and Trade
GB	Great Britain
GBE	Knight (or Dame) Grand Cross, Order of British Empire
GBH	grievous bodily harm
GC	George Cross; Group Captain
GCB	Knight Grand Cross, Order of the Bath
GCE	General Certificate of Education
gcf	greatest common factor
GCH	Knight Grand Cross of Hanover (obsolete)
GCIE	Knight Grand Commander, Order of Indian Empire
GCLH	Grand Cross of Legion of Honour
gcm	greatest common measure
GCMG	Knight (or Dame) Grand Cross of St Michael and St George (Order)
GCSI	Knight Grand Commander, Star of India (Order)
GCVO	Knight (or Dame) Grand Cross, Royal Victorian Order
Gdsm	Guardsman
GEC	General Electric Company
Gen	Genesis; General
gen	gender; genitive; general; information (slang)
GFTU	General Federation of Trade Unions
GG	Girl Guides; Governor General
GHQ	General Headquarters
GInst MSM	Graduate of Institute of Marketing and Sales Management
GLC	Greater London Council
GLCM	Graduate of London College of Music
GM	George Medal; Grand Master
GMB	Great Master, Order of the Bath
GMBE	Grand Master, Order of the British Empire

GMC	General Medical Council
GMMG	Grand Master, Order of St Michael and St George
GMT	Greenwich Mean Time
GMVO	Grand Master, Royal Victorian Order
GOC	General Officer Commanding
Gov	Governor
GP	General Practitioner
GPh	Graduate in Pharmacy
GPI	General Paralysis of the Insane
GPO	General Post Office
GQG	Grand Quartier General = GHQ (French)
GR	(*Georgius Rex*) King George; (*Gulielmus Rex*) King William; Grand Recorder
GRCM	Graduate Royal College of Music
GRSM	Graduate Royal School of Music
gs	grandson
GSM	Guildhall School of Music
GSO	General Staff Officer

H

H	Harbour; hard (of pencils); hydrant
h	hour, hours; husband; hundred
HA	Horse Artillery; Hockey Association
ha	(*hoc anno*) this year; (*hujus anni*) this year's; heir apparent
HAC	Honourable Artillery Company
HB	hard and black (of pencils)
HBM	His (or Her) Britannic Majesty
HC	House of Commons; High Church; Habitual Criminal
hcf	highest common factor
HE	His (or Her) Excellency
HEH	His (or Her) Exalted Highness
HFRA	Honorary Fellow of the Royal Academy
HG	His (or Her) Grace; Home Guard; Horse Guards; High German
HH	His (or Her) Highness; extra hard (of pencils)
hhd	hogshead
HI	(*hic jacet*) here lies
Hib	Hibernian
HIH	His (or Her) Imperial Highness
Hil	Hilary term
HIM	His (or Her) Imperial Majesty

HJS	(*hic jacet sepultus*) here lies buried
HL	House of Lords
HLI	Highland Light Infantry
HM	His (or Her) Majesty
HMAS	Her Majesty's Australian Ship
HMCS	Her Majesty's Canadian Ship
HMI	Her Majesty's Inspector
HMIS	Her Majesty's Indian Ship
HML	Her Majesty's Lieutenant
HMS	Her Majesty's Ship
HMSO	Her Majesty's Stationery Office
Hon	Honourable; Honorary
HP	Hire Purchase; Half pay
hp	horse power, heir presumptive
HQ	Headquarters
HRH	His (or Her) Royal Highness
HSE	(*hic sepultus est*) here lies buried
HSH	His (or Her) Serene Highness
Hum	(*humaniora*) the humanities
hw	hit wicket (cricket)
HWM	High Water Mark
hyd	hydrant; hydrostatics

I

I	Ireland; island; isle; (*Imperator*) Emperor; (*Imperatrix*) Empress
IA	Indian Army; Incorporated Accountant
IAAA	Irish Amateur Athletic Association
IAAM	Incorporated Association of Assistant Masters
IAEA	International Atomic Energy Agency
IALPA	International Air Line Pilots Assocn.
IARO	Indian Army Reserve of Officers
IB	Intelligence Branch
ib (ibid)	(*Ibidem*) in the same place
IBRD	International Bank for Reconstruction and Development (World Bank)
ICAO	International Civil Aviation Organisation
ICBM	Inter-Continental Ballistic Missile
ICE	Institution of Civil Engineers
ICI	Imperial Chemical Industries
ICJ	International Court of Justice
ICS	Indian Civil Service
ICY	Imperial Cadet Yeomanry
ID	Intelligence Department
id	(*idem*) the same

IDA	International Development Association
IDB	Illicit diamond buyer
IDC	Imperial Defence College
ie	(*id est*) that is
IEE	Institution of Electrical Engineers
IFC	International Finance Corporation
IG	Inspector-General
IGY	International Geophysical Year
IHS	(*Jesus Hominum Salvator*) Jesus Saviour of Man
ILO	International Labour Organisation
ILP	Independent Labour Party
ILS	Incorporated Law Society
IMA	Indian Military Academy
IMCO	Inter-Governmental Maritime Consultative Organisation
IMD	Indian Medical Department
IMF	International Monetary Fund
IMNS	Imperial Military Nursing Service
IMS	Indian Medical Service
in	inch
INA	Institution of Naval Architects
Inc	Incorporated
incog	(*incognito*) unknown, not under own name
Ind	Independent
Infra	below
in lim	(*in limine*) at the outset
in loc	(*in loco*) in its place
INRI	(*Jesus Nazarenus Rex Judaeorum*) Jesus of Nazareth, King of the Jews
inst	(instant) this current month
Inst Act	Institute of Actuaries
Inst CE	Institution of Civil Engineers
Inst EE	Institution of Electrical Engineers
Inst ME	Institution of Marine Engineers
Inst MechE	Institution of Mechanical Engineers
IOGT	International Order of Good Templars
IOM	Isle of Man; Indian Order of Merit
IOOF	Independent Order of Oddfellows
IOP	Institute of Painters in Water Colours
IOW	Isle of Wight
IQ	Intelligence Quota
IRA	Irish Republican Army
IRBM	Intermediate Range Ballistic Missile
IRC	Industrial Reorganisation Corporation
IRO	Inland Revenue Office
ISC	Indian Staff College (Corps)

ISM	Imperial Service Medal; Incorporated Society of Musicians
ISO	Companion of Imperial Service Order
ITA	Independent Television Authority
Ital	*italic* type
ITC	Infantry Training Centre
ITO	International Trade Organisation
ITU	International Telecommunication Union
ITV	Independent Television

J

J	(Mr) Justice
JA	Judge-Advocate
JAG	Judge-Advocate-General
Jas.	James
JD	Junior Deacon
JGTC	Junior Girls Training Corps
JIC	Joint Industrial Council
JJ	Justices
Jno	John
JP	Justice of the Peace
JR	(*Jacobus Rex*) King James
Jr	Junior
JTC	Junior Training Corps
JUD	(*Juris utriusque Doctor*) Doctor of both civil and canon law

K

KAR	King's African Rifles
KB	Knight of the Bath (Order)
KBE	Knight Commander of the British Empire (Order)
KCB	Knight Commander of the Bath (Order)
KCIE	Knight Commander of the Indian Empire (Order)
KCL	King's College, London
KCMG	Knight Commander of St Michael and St George (Order)
KCSI	Knight Commander of Star of India (Order)
KCVO	Knight Commander of Royal Victorian Order
KG	Knight of the (Order of the) Garter
KGStJ	Knight of Grace, St John of Jerusalem (Order)
KHC	King's Honorary Chaplain
KHP	King's Honorary Physician
KHS	King's Honorary Surgeon; Knight of Holy Sepulchre

KiH	Kaisar-i-Hind Medal
KJStJ	Knight of Justice, St John of Jerusalem (Order)
KKK	Ku-Klux-Klan
KM	Knight of Malta
ko	knock-out
KORR	King's Own Royal Regiment
KOSB	King's Own Scottish Borderers
KOYLI	King's Own Yorkshire Light Infantry
KP	Knight of (Order of) St Patrick
KRR	King's Royal Rifles
KRRC	King's Royal Rifle Corps
KS	King's Scholar
KSG	Knight of St Gregory
KT	Knight of (Order of) the Thistle
Kt	Knight (Bachelor)

L

L	Liberal; Pound (money); Lake; London
LA	Library Association; Legislative Assembly
Lab	Labour
LAC	Leading Aircraftman; London Athletic Club
LAM	(*Liberalium Artium Magister*) Master of the Liberal Arts; London Academy of Music
LAMDA	London Academy of Music and Dramatic Art
lat	latitude
lb	(*libra*) pound (weight)
lbw	leg before wicket (cricket)
LC	Lord Chancellor; Lord Chamberlain; left centre; Legislative Council
lc	lower case—small letters (printing); (*loco citato*) in the place cited
LCC	London County Council (now GLC)
LCJ	Lord Chief Justice
LCorp	Lance-Corporal
lcm	least common multiple
LEB	London Electricity Board
LFB	London Fire Brigade
LGU	Ladies Golf Union
LH	(play with) left hand (*music*)
LHA	Lord High Admiral
LHD	(*Literarium Humaniorum Doctor*) Doctor of Literature
LI	Light Infantry
Lib	(*liber*) Book; Liberal

*   *   *

LICENTIATES	LICENTIATE (of, or in)
LAH	Apothecaries Hall, Dublin
LCh	Surgery
LCP	College of Preceptors
LDiv	Divinity
LDS	Dental Surgery
LFPS	Faculty of Physicians and Surgeons
LGSM	Guildhall School of Music
LLCM	London College of Music
LM	Midwifery
LMSSA	Medicine and Surgery, Society of Apothecaries (London)
LRAM	Royal Academy of Music
LRCM	Royal College of Music
LRCP	Royal College of Physicians
LRCVS	Royal College of Veterinary Surgeons
LRFPSG	Royal Faculty of Physicians and Surgeons, Glasgow
LRIBA	Royal Institute of British Architects
LSA	Society of Apothecaries (London)
LTCL	Trinity College of Music, London
LTh	Theology
LTM	Tropical Medicine
LTSC	Tonic Sol-Fa College (of Music)

*   *   *

Lieut	Lieutenant
lin	lineal; linear
Lit	Literature; literally
LitD	Doctor of Letters
Lit Hum	(*Literae Humaniores*) Classics—final school (= examination) at Oxford
Litt D	Doctor of Letters (or Literature)
LJ	Lord Justice
LL	Laws
LLA	Lady Literate in Arts
LLB	Bachelor of Laws
LLD	Doctor of Laws
LLM	Master of Civil and Canon Law
LMR	London Midland Region
LO	London Office; Liaison Officer
L of C	Lines of Communication
loc cit	(*loco citato*) in the place cited
long	longitude
Lp	Lordship; long-player (record)
LRB	London Rifle Brigade

LS	(*loco sigilli*) place of the seal; Leading seaman
Lsd	(*librae, solidi, denarii*) pounds, shillings and pence; money; lysergic acid
LSE	London School of Economics
LSO	London Symphony Orchestra
LTA	Lawn Tennis Association
Lt	Lieutenant
LTB	London Transport Board
Ltd	Limited (liability)
LU	Liberal Unionist
LXX	The Septuagint (Bible)
Ly	Lady

M

M	Majesty; Marquess (or Marquis); (*mille*) 1000
m	male; masculine; married; mile; metre; million; maiden over (cricket)
mA	milliampere
MAA	Master-at-Arms
M and D	Medicine and Duty

*   *   *

MASTERS	MASTER (of)
MA	Arts
MAO	Obstetrics
MArch	Architecture
MAS	Applied Science
MCh	Surgery
MChD	Dental Surgery
MChOrth	Orthopaedic Surgery
MCL	Civil Law
MCom	Commerce
MDS	Dental Surgery
MEng	Engineering
MFA	Fine Arts, Fox Hounds
MH (MHy)	Hygiene
MMet	Metallurgy
MMusRCM	Music, Royal College of Music
MMSA	Midwifery of the Society of Apothecaries
MS	Surgery
MSc	Science
MSD	Surgeon Dentist
MTh	Theology
MusM	Music
MVSc	Veterinary Science

*   *   *

MAB	Metropolitan Asylums Board
Maj	Major
MB	Bachelor of Medicine
Mbr	Member
MC	Military Cross; Master of Ceremonies
MCC	Marylebone Cricket Club
MD	Doctor of Medicine
Md	(*mano destra* or *main droit*) with the right hand (*music*)

*   *   *

MEMBERS	MEMBER of the
MAA	Advertising Association
MAI	Anthropological Institute
M Am Soc CE	Amalgamated Society of Civil Engineers
MAOT	Association of Occupational Therapists
MBE	Order of the British Empire
MBIM	British Institute of Management
MBOU	British Ornithologists Union
MCMES	Civil and Mechanical Engineers Society
MCP	Colonial Parliament; College of Preceptors
MCSP	Chartered Society of Physiotherapists
MEC	Executive Council
MEIC	Engineering Institute of Canada
MGI	Institute of Certificated Grocers
MHA	House of Assembly
MHK	House of Keys
MIAE	Institute of Automobile Engineers
MIAMA	Incorporated Advertising Managers Association
MICE	Institute of Civil Engineers
MIChemE	Institute of Chemical Engineers
MIEE	Institute of Electrical Engineers
MIFireE	Institute of Fire Engineers
MIHVE	Institution of Heating & Ventilating Engineers
MILocoE	Institute of Locomotive Engineers
MIMarE	Institute of Marine Engineers
MIMechE	Institution of Mechanical Engineers
MIMinE	Institution of Mining Engineers
MIMM	Institute of Mining and Metallurgy
MIMT	Institute of the Motor Trade
MINA	Institution of Naval Architects
MInstBE	Institute of British Engineers
MInstCE	Institution of Civil Engineers
MInstGasE	Institution of Gas Engineers

MInstMM	Institute of Mining and Metallurgy
MInstMet	Institute of Metals
MInstMSM	Institute of Marketing and Sales Management
MInstNA	Institution of Naval Architects
MInstPT	Institute of Petroleum Technologists
MInst RA	Institute of Registered Architects
MInstT	Institute of Transport
MInstWE	Institution of Water Engineers
MIOB	Institute of Builders
MIOM	Institute of Office Management
MIPA	Institute of Practitioners in Advertising
MIPE	Institution of Production Engineers
MIPM	Institute of Personnel Management
MIPR	Institute of Public Relations
MITA	Industrial Transport Association
MISI	Iron and Steel Institute
MIStructE	Institution of Structural Engineers
MIWM	Institution of Works Managers
MIWT	Institute of Wireless Technology
MJI	Institute of Journalists
MLA	Legislative Assembly
MLC	Legislative Council
MLSC	London Society of Compositors
MP	Parliament
MPC	Parliament of Canada
MPP	Provincial Parliament
MPS	Pharmaceutical Society; Philological Society; Physical Society
MRAeS	Royal Aeronautical Society
MRAC	Royal Agricultural College
MRAS	Royal Asian Society; Royal Academy of Science
MRCC	Royal College of Chemistry
MRCO	Royal College of Organists
MRCOG	Royal College of Obstetricians and Gynaecologists
MRCP	Royal College of Physicians
MRCS	Royal College of Surgeons
MRCVS	Royal College of Veterinary Surgeons
MRI	Royal Institution
MRIA	Royal Irish Academy
MRO	Register of Osteopaths
MRSanI	Royal Sanitary Institute
MRST	Royal Society of Teachers
MRUSI	Royal United Service Institute
MSA	Society of Architects

MSI	Chartered Surveyors' Institution
MSRG	Society of Remedial Gymnasts
MTPI	Town Planning Institute
MVO	Royal Victorian Order

*   *   *

ME	Middle English
MEF	Mediterranean Expeditionary Force
Messrs	(*Messieurs*) Gentlemen; Sirs; plural of Mister
mf	more following; *mezzo-forte*, rather loud (*music*)
MG	(*main gauche*) with the left hand (*music*)
MGO	Master General of Ordnance
Mgr	Monsignor
Mlle	(*Mademoiselle*) Miss
Min	Minister; Ministry
Min Tech	Ministry of Technology
MM	Military Medal; Mercantile Marine; *Messieurs*
Mme	(*Madame*) Mrs
MN	Merchant Navy
MO	Medical Officer; Money Order
MOD	Ministry of Defence
Mods	Moderations (Oxford examinations)
MOH	Medical Officer of Health; Master of Otter-hounds; Ministry of Health
MOI	Ministry of Information
MOT	Ministry of Transport
MP	Member of Parliament
mph	miles per hour
MR	Master of the Rolls
Mr	Master; Mister
MRA	Moral Re-Armament
MRAF	Marshal of the Royal Air Force
Mrs	Mistress; 'Missis'
MRC	Medical Research Council
MS (MSS)	Manuscript (Manuscripts); (*mano sinistra*) with the left hand (*music*)
MSC	Metropolitan Special Constabulary
MSH	Master of Staghounds
MSM	Meritorious Service Medal
Mt	Mount; Mountain
MTB	Motor Torpedo Boat
Mus B	Bachelor of Music
Mus D	Doctor of Music
Mus M	Master of Music
MWB	Metropolitan Water Board

N

N	North; Note; Nationalist; Nitrogen
NA	National Academy or Academician; National Assistance
NAAFI	Navy, Army and Air Force Institute
NALGO	National Association of Local Government Officers
NASD	National Amalgamated Stevedores and Dockers (Union)
Nat	National; natural
NATO	North Atlantic Treaty Organisation
NB	(*Nota bene*) note well
NBS	National Broadcasting Service
NCB	National Coal Board
NCC	Non-Combatant Corps
NCO	Non-commissioned officer
NCU	National Cyclists Union
NCW	National Council of Women
nd	No date (of publication)
NDA	National Diploma in Agriculture
NDC	National Defence Corps
NE	North-East; New England
NEDC	National Economic Development Council
NEL	National Engineering Laboratory
nem con	(*nemine contradicente*) no one contradicting
nem diss	(*nemine dissentiente*) no one dissenting
NFS	National Fire Service
NFU	National Farmers' Union
NHRU	National Home Reading Union
NHS	National Health Service
NI	Native Infantry
NID	Naval Intelligence Division
NIRA	National Industrial Recovery Act
NL and C	National Liberal and Conservative
NLF	National Liberal Federation
NNE	North-North-East
NNW	North-North-West
NO	Naval Officer; Navigation Officer
no	number
NOD	Naval Ordnance Department
nom	nominative; nominal
non seq	(*non sequitur*) It does not follow
NOP	National Opinion Poll
nos	numbers
NP	Notary Public; new paragraph

NPD	National Democratic Party (German)
NRA	National Rifle Association
NS	New Style (calendar); National Society
NSA	National Swimming (or Skating) Association
NSC	National Savings Committee; National Sporting Club
NSPCC	National Society for the Prevention of Cruelty to Children
NSW	New South Wales
NT	New Testament
NUJ	National Union of Journalists
NUM	National Union of Mineworkers
NUR	National Union of Railwaymen
NUS	National Union of Students
NUT	National Union of Teachers
NUTN	National Union of Trained Nurses
NUWT	National Union of Women Teachers
NUWW	National Union of Women Workers
NW	North-West
NWMP	North-West Mounted Police (Canadian)
NWP(T)	North-West Province (Territory)
NY	New York
NZ	New Zealand

O

O	Order; old; oxygen
OA	Ordnance Artificer
o/a	on account
OB	Outside Broadcast
ob	(*obiit*) died
OBE	Officer of the Order of the British Empire
obit	Obituary
obs	obsolete
OC	Officer Commanding
OCTU	Officer Cadet Training Unit
OE	Old English
OECD	Organisation for Economic Co-operation and Development
OED	Oxford English Dictionary
OEEC	Organisation for European Economic Co-operation
OFM	Order of Friars Minor
OHBMS	On His (or Her) Britannic Majesty's Service

OHMS	On His (or Her) Majesty's Service; (Oberkommando des Herres) Army High Command (German)
OKL	(Oberkommando der Luftwaffe) Air Force High Command (German)
OKM	(Oberkommando der Kriegsmarine) Navy High Command (German)
OM	Order of Merit
OME	Ordnance Mechanical Engineer
OMI	Oblate of Mary Immaculate
ONC	Ordinary National Certificate
OND	Ordinary National Diploma
OP	Order of Preachers; Opposite Prompt (theatre); Out of Print (book); over proof (spirits)
op	(*opus*) work
op cit	(*opere citato*) in the work cited
ORC	Order of the Red Cross
Ord	Ordnance; ordinary
Orse	Otherwise
OS	Ordnance Survey; Ordinary Seaman
OSA	Order of St Augustine
OSB	Order of St Benedict
OSD	Order of St Dominic; Ordnance Survey Dept.
OSFC	Order of St Francis (Capuchin)
OT	Old Testament
OTC	Officers' Training Corps
OU	Oxford University
Oxon	Oxford (University); Oxfordshire
Oz	ounce
OUBC	Oxford University Boat Club
OUDS	Oxford University Dramatic Society

P

P	Page; Pastor; Father; Prince; Pawn (chess)
p	(piano) soft (*music*); page
PA	Personal Assistant; Post Adjutant; Protestant Alliance; Press Association (news agency)
P/A	Power of Attorney
pa	(*per annum*) yearly; by the year
PAADC	Principal Air Aide-de-Camp
P & O	Peninsular and Oriental Steam Navigation Co.
Parlt	Parliament
Parly	Parliamentary

PASI	Professional Associate of the Chartered Surveyors' Institution
PAYE	Pay As You Earn (tax)
PBI	infantryman (military slang)
PC	Privy Councillor (or Counsellor); Police Constable
PCMO	Principal Colonial Medical Officer
PD	Preventive Detention
pd	paid
PDSA	People's Dispensary for Sick Animals
PEN	Poets, Essayists and Novelists (Club)
per cent	(*per centum*) by (or in) the hundred
per pro	(*per procurationem*) by proxy
PF	Procurator Fiscal
pf	(*pour féliciter*) to congratulate; post free
pfc	Passed Flying College
PhB	Bachelor of Philosophy
PhC	Pharmaceutical Chemist (American)
PhD	Doctor of Philosophy
Phil Soc	Philological Society of London
pinx	(*pinxit*) he (or she) painted it
PJ	Probate Judge; presiding judge
Pk	Park
PKTF	Printing and Kindred Trades Federation
PL	Paymaster Lieutenant
P/L	Profit and Loss
Pl	Plural
PLA	Port of London Authority
Plen	Plenipotentiary
PLUTO	Pipe Line Under the Ocean
PM	(*post meridiem*) afternoon; (*post mortem*) after death; Prime Minister; Past Master
PMG	Postmaster-General; Paymaster-General
PMO	Principal Medical Officer
PMRAFNS	Princess Mary's Royal Air Force Nursing Service
PNEU	Parents' National Educational Union
PO	Post Office; postal order; petty officer
POO	Principal Ordnance Officer
pop	population; popularly
PoW	Prisoner of War
pp	(see *per pro*); pianissimo (very softly) (*music*); past participle; post paid; pages; parcel post
PPC	(*pour prendre congé*) to take leave
PPRA	Past President of the Royal Academy
PPS	Parliamentary Private Secretary

PR	Public Relations
PRA	President of the Royal Academy
PRCA	President of the Royal Cambrian Academy
Preb	Prebendary
prep	preparation; preparatory; preposition
Pres	President; presiding
PRHA	President of the Royal Hibernian Academy
PRI	President of the Royal Institute (of Painters in Water Colours)
Prin	Principal
PRO	Public Relations Officer
pro	for, in favour of; in place of; professional
Prof	Professor
pro tem	(*pro tempore*) for the time being
Prom	Promenade
pron	pronoun; pronunciation; pronounced
Prop	Propose; proposal
Prot	Protestant
Prov	Proverbs; provincial; Provost
prov	provisional; provincial
prox	(*proximo*) next (usually next month)
PRS	President of the Royal Society
PRSA	President of the Royal Scottish Academy
PRSE	President of the Royal Society of Edinburgh
PS	(*post scriptum*) postscript; Permanent Secretary; Police Sergeant; Prompt Side (theatre)
Ps	Psalms
psc	Passed Staff College
PT	Physical Training
Pt	Part; point
PTA	Parent–Teacher Association
Pte	Private (soldier)
PTO	please turn over
Pty	Proprietary (company)
pub	public; published
Pvt	Private (American soldier)
PWD	Public Works Department

Q

Q	Queen; question; quire
q	(*quaere*) Inquire; query; quasi
QAIMNS	Queen Alexandra's Imperial Military Nursing Service
QARANC	Queen Alexandra's Royal Army Nursing Corps

QARNNS	Queen Alexandra's Royal Naval Nursing Service
QALAS	Qualified Associate of the Land Agents' Society
QB	Queen's Bench
QC	Queen's Counsel; Queen's College
qd	(*quasi dicat*) as if one should say; (*Quasi dictum*) as if said
QE	Queen Elizabeth (liner)
qe	(*quod est*) which is
QED	(*quod erat demonstrandum*) which was to be proved
QEF	(*quod erat faciendum*) which was to be done
QEI	(*quod erat inveniendum*) which was to be found out
QF	quick firing
QFSM	Queen's Fire Service Medal
QHC	Queen's Honorary Chaplain
QHDS	Queen's Honorary Dental Surgeon
QHNS	Queen's Honorary Nursing Sister
QHP	Queen's Honorary Physician
QHS	Queen's Honorary Surgeon
QL	(*quantum libet*) as much as you please
QM	Quartermaster
QMG	Quartermaster-General
QMS	Quartermaster-Sergeant
Qn	Queen; question
QOCH	Queen's Own Cameron Highlanders
q pl	(*quantum placet*) as much as seems good
QPM	Queen's Police Medal
qr	quarter; quire
QSO	Quasi-stellar Object
qt	quart; quantity
qu	question
quad	quadrant; quadrangle
qv	(*quod vide*) which see; (*quantum vis*) as much as you will
QVR	Queen Victoria Rifles
Qy	query

R

R	(*Rex*) King; (*Regina*) Queen; Rector; Rabbi; Royal; railway; registered; reply; river; rouble; right
RA	Rear-Admiral

RAFO	Reserve of Air Force Officers
Rall.	(*rallentando*) slower (*music*)
RB	Rifle Brigade
RC	Roman Catholic; Red Cross
RD	Rural Dean; Refer to Drawer (cheque)
RDC	Rural District Council
RDI	Designer for Industry, Royal Society of Arts
RE	Fellow of Royal Society of Painter Etchers
rec'd	received
Ref	Reformed; reference
Reg	(*Regina*) Queen; Registered
Rep	Republic; Repertory; Representative
Rev	Reverend; Revelation
RH	Royal Highness
Rhet	Rhetoric
RIP	(*Requiescat in pace*) May he (or she) rest in peace
Rit.	(*ritenuto*) hold back (*music*)
RM	Resident Magistrate
Ro	(*recto*) on the right-hand page
RMN	Registered Mental Nurse
RNMS	Registered Nurse for Mentally Subnormal

*   *   *

ROYAL

RA	Academy; Academician; Artillery
RAA	Academy of Arts
RAAF	Australian Air Force
RAC	Automobile Club; Armoured Corps; Agricultural College
RAChD	Army Chaplains Department
RADA	Academy of Dramatic Art
RADC	Army Dental Corps
RAEC	Army Educational Corps
RAeC	Aero Club
RAeS	Aeronautical Society
RAF	Air Force
RAFA	Air Forces Association
RAFES	Air Force Educational Service
RAFR	Air Force Regiment
RAFVR	Air Force Volunteer Reserve
RAM	Academy of Music (London)
RAMC	Army Medical Corps
RAN	Australian Navy
RAuxAF	Auxiliary Air Force
RAOB	Antediluvian Order of Buffaloes

RAOC	Army Ordnance Corps
RAPC	Army Pay Corps
RAS	Astronomical Society; Asiatic Society
RASC	Army Service Corps
RAVC	Army Veterinary Corps
RBA	Society of British Artists
RBS	Society of British Sculptors
RCA	Cambrian Academician
RCAF	Canadian Air Force
RCMP	Canadian Mounted Police
RCN	Canadian Navy
RCNC	Corps of Naval Constructors
RCO	College of Organists
RCP	College of Physicians
RCS	College of Surgeons; College of Science
RCT	Corps of Transport
RCVS	College of Veterinary Surgeons
RDC	Defence Corps
RDI	Designer for Industry
RDS	Drawing Society
RE	Engineers
REME	Electrical and Mechanical Engineers
RFA	Field Artillery
RGA	Garrison Artillery
RGS	Geographical Society
RHA	Horse Artillery; Hibernian Academy
RHG	Horse Guards
RHistS	Historical Society
RHMS	Hibernian Military School
RHS	Horticultural Society; Humane Society
RI	Institute of Painters in Water Colours
RIA	Irish Academy
RIASC	Indian Army Service Corps
RIBA	Institute of British Architects
RIBS	Institute of British Sculptors
RIC	Institute of Chemistry
RIEC	Indian Engineering College
RIIA	Institute of International Affairs
RIM	Indian Marine
RIN	Indian Navy
RLSS	Life Saving Society
RM	Marines; Mail
RMA	Marine Artillery; Military Academy (Sandhurst)
RMC	Military College
RMetS	Meteorological Society

RMLI	Marine Light Infantry
RMP	Corps of Military Police
RMS	Microscopical Society; Society of Miniature Painters; Mail Steamer
RMSM	Military School of Music
RN	Navy
RNAS	Naval Air Service
RND	Naval Reserve Decoration
RNLI	National Lifeboat Institution
RNR	Naval Reserve
RNVR	Naval Volunteer Reserve
RNVSR	Naval Volunteer Supplementary Reserve
RNZAF	New Zealand Air Force
RNZN	New Zealand Navy
ROC	Observer Corps
ROI	Institute of Oil Painters
RoSPA	Society for Prevention of Accidents
RP	Society of Portrait Painters
RPC	Pioneer Corps; Pay Corps
RPS	Photographic Society
RRC	Red Cross (Order, Member of)
RRW	Regiment of Wales
RS	Signals
RSA	Scottish Academician (or Academy); Society of Arts
RSAAF	South African Air Force
RSD	Society of Dublin
RSE	Society of Edinburgh
RSF	Scots Fusiliers
R Sigs	Signals
RSL	Society of Literature
RSM	School of Mines; Society of Medicine
RSPB	Society for the Protection of Birds
RSPCA	Society for the Prevention of Cruelty to Animals
RSWS	Scottish Water Colour Society
RTC	Tank Corps
RTR	Tank Regiment
RTS	Toxophilite Society
RTYC	Thames Yacht Club
RUC	Ulster Constabulary
RUR	Ulster Rifles
RUSI	United Service Institution
RVC	Victorian Chain
RVCI	Veterinary College of Ireland
RWF	Welsh Fusiliers

RWS	Society of Painters in Water Colours
RYS	Yacht Squadron (club)

*   *   *

RPD	(*Rerum Politicarum Doctor*) Doctor of Political Science
rpm	revolutions per minute
RSFSR	Russian Socialist Federated Soviet Republic
RSGB	Reform Synagogues of Great Britain
RSM	Regimental Sergeant Major; Resident Stage Manager
RSS	(*Regiae Societatis Sodis*) Fellow of Royal Society
RSVP	(*Répondez s'il vous plaît*) Reply, if you please
RT	Radio Telephone
Rt Hon	Right Honourable
Rt Rev	Right Reverend
Rt Wpfl	Right Worshipful
RTO	Railway Transport Officer
RV	Revised Version (Bible); Rifle Volunteers

S

S	South; Saint; Saxon; Socialist; Sabbath; Society
s	(*solidus, solidi*) shilling, shillings; second, seconds; son; singular; substantive; succeeded
SACEUR	Supreme Allied Commander, Europe
SA	(*Société Anonyme*) French equivalent of 'Ltd'; South Africa; South America; Salvation Army; Sex Appeal
SAE	Society of Automobile Engineers
Sae	Stamped addressed envelope
Salop	Shropshire
Sans	Sanskrit; sanserif (printing type)
SAR	Search and Rescue Centre (Civil Aviation)
SAS	Special Air Service (Regiment)
SASC	Small Arms School Corps
SASO	Senior Air Staff Office
SAVR	Special Army Volunteer Reserve
SBAC	Society of British Aircraft Constructors
SC	State Counsel; Staff College
Sc	(*scilicet*) namely; (*sculpsit*) he (she) engraved it
SCAPA	Society for Checking Abuses of Public Advertising
ScB	Bachelor of Science

ScD	Doctor of Science
Sch	school; schedule
SCL	Student of Civil Law
SCM	State Certified Midwife; Student Christian Movement
ScM	Master of Science
SCWS	Scottish Co-operative Wholesale Society
SE	South-East
SEATO	South-East Asia Treaty Organisation
Sec	Secretary; second
Sect	Section
Sen (Senr)	Senior
SEN	State Enrolled Nurse
Seq	(*sequellae*) the following
Ser	Service
SFS	Scouts Friendly Society
SG	Solicitor General; Scots Guards
Sgt	Sergeant
SHAEF	Supreme Headquarters Allied Expeditionary Force
SHAPE	Supreme Headquarters Allied Powers Europe
SIA	Society of Industrial Artists
sic	(*sic*) thus; so written
sin	(*sinistra*) to be played with left hand (*music*)
sing	singular
SJ	Society of Jesus (Jesuits)
Sjt	Serjeant
SL	Serjeant-at-Law
SM	Stage Manager
SME	School of Military Engineering
SMMT	Society of Motor Manufacturers and Traders
SNO	Senior Naval Officer
Socy (So., Soc)	Society
SOE	Special Operations Executive
SOGAT	Society of Graphical and Allied Trades
Sol	solution; soluble
Solr	solicitor
SOME	Senior Ordnance Mechanical Engineer
SOS	Distress signal 'Save Our Souls'
sp	(*sine prole*) without issue; childless
SPCK	Society for Promoting Christian Knowledge
SPG	Society for the Propagation of the Gospel
SPQR	(*Senatus Populusque Romanus*) Senate and People of Rome
SPR	Society for Psychical Research
SPRC	Society for Prevention and Relief of Cancer

SPRL	Society for Promotion of Religion and Learning
SPSP	St Peter and St Paul (The Papal Seal)
SPVD	Society for the Prevention of Venereal Disease
Sq	square
SR	Special Reserve; Southern Region
Sr	senior
SRD	State Registered Dietitian
SRI	(*Sacrum Romanum Imperium*) The Holy Roman Empire
SRN	State Registered Nurse
SRO	Special Reserve of Officers
SS	Saints; steam ship; Secretary of State; Straits Settlements; Sunday School; screw steamer
SSAFA	Soldiers', Sailors' and Airmen's Families Association
SSC	Solicitor before the Supreme Courts (Scotland)
SSE	South-South-East
SSJE	Society of St John the Evangelist
SSM	Society of the Sacred Mission
SSU	Sunday School Union
SSW	South-South-West
St	Saint; street
STB	Bachelor of Sacred Theology
STD	Doctor of Sacred Theology; subscriber trunk dialling
Stet	(*stet*) let it stand
Stg	sterling
STP	Professor of Sacred Theology
Sub	Sub-editor; substitute
Subs	Substantive
Sup	superior
Supt	Superintendent; supplement
Surg	Surgeon
Svce	Service
SW	South-West; South Wales
SWO	Squadron Wireless Operator (Naval)

T

T	Territory; temperature; Testament
t	ton, tons; town, township; (*tempore*) in the time of
TA	Territorial Army
TAA	Territorial Army Association
TAN	Twilight All Night
tan	tangents

TB	Tuberculosis; Torpedo Boat
T & AF Assn	Territorial and Auxiliary Forces Association
TCD	Trinity College, Dublin
TD	Territorial (Officer's) Decoration
Text Rec	(*Textus receptus*) Received text
TF	Territorial Force
TGWU	Transport and General Workers' Union
Theol	Theology
Thess	Thessalonians
TIH	Their Imperial Highnesses
Tit	title
TNT	Trinitrotoluene (explosive)
Toc H	Talbot House
Tr	Translator; translation; translated; transport
TRC	Thames Rowing Club; Tithes Rent Charge
TRH	Their Royal Highnesses
Trin	Trinity
TSD	Tertiary of St Dominick
TSH	Their Serene Highnesses
TSSA	Transport Salaried Staffs Association
TUC	Trades Union Congress/Council
TVA	Tennessee Valley Authority (US)
TWV	Transport Workers' Union
TYC	Thames Yacht Club
Typ	Typography; typographer; typographical

U

U	Unionist; University; Uranium
UC	University College
uc	upper case (Capitals, in printing)
UDC	Urban District Council; Union of Democratic Control
UF	United Free (Church of Scotland)
UFO	Unidentified Flying Object
uhf	ultra high frequency (waves)
UK	United Kingdom
ult	(*ultimo*) in the preceding month; last month
UN	United Nations
UNA	United Nations Association
UNAC	United Nations Appeal for Children
UNCTAD	United Nations Conference on Trade and Development
UNESCO	United Nations Educational, Scientific and Cultural Organisation
UNICEF	United Nations International Children's Emergency Fund

UNIDO	United Nations Industrial Development Organisation
Univ	University
UNO	United Nations Organisation
UNREF	United Nations Refugee Emergency Fund
UNRRA	United Nations Relief and Rehabilitation Administration
UP	United Provinces; Uttar Pradesh
up	under proof (spirits)
UPU	Universal Postal Union
UPC	United Presbyterian Church
US	United States; United Service
us	(*ubi supra*) in the place above-mentioned; (*ut supra*) as above
USA	United States of America
USAC	United States Air Corps
USCL	United Society for Christian Literature
USDAW	Union of Shop, Distributive and Allied Workers
USM	United States Marines
USMA	United States Military Academy
USN	United States Navy
USNA	United States Naval Academy
USS	United States Ship; US Senator (or Senate)
USSC	United States Supreme Court
USSR	Union of Soviet Socialist Republics (Russian)
USV	United States Volunteers
ut dict	(*ut dictum*) as directed
ut sup	(*ut supra*) as above
UU	University Union
U/w	Underwriter
ux	(*uxor*) wife

V

V	Viscount; five; volt; Vice-
V1, V2	Vergeltungswaffe (German for 'reprisal weapon')
v	(*versus*) against; (*vide*) see; verse; volt; verb; voice; violin
VA	Royal Order of Victoria and Albert (Lady of the); Vicar Apostolic
V & A	Victoria and Albert (Museum)
VAD	Voluntary Aid Detachment
Vb	Verb
VC	Victoria Cross; Vice-Chancellor; Vice-Chairman

VCAS	Vice-Chief of Air Staff
VCIGS	Vice-Chief of the Imperial General Staff
VD	Volunteer Officers' Decoration; Venereal Disease
VDM	(*verbi Dei Minister*) Minister of the Word of God
VE	Victory in Europe (VE Day was May 8, 1945)
Ven	Venerable
Verb sap	(*verbum sapienti satis est*) a word to the wise is enough
Vet	Veterinary (surgeon or officer)
vhf	very high frequency (radio waves)
vi	verb intransitive
Vice-Adm	Vice-Admiral
VIP	Very Important Person
Visct	Viscount
viz	(*videlicet*) namely
VJ	Victory over Japan (VJ Day, August 15, 1945)
VMH	Victoria Medal of Honour (Horticulture)
vo	(*verso*) on the left-hand page
Voc	vocative; vocal
Vol	Volume; volunteer(s); voluntary
VP	Vice-President
VR	(*Victoria Regina*) Queen Victoria
VRC	Volunteer Rifle Corps
VRD	RNVR Officer's Decoration
VRI	(*Victoria Regina et Imperatrix*) Victoria, Queen and Empress (India)
vt	verb transitive
Vulg	The Vulgate (Bible)
vulg	vulgar, vulgarly; vulgar, vulgarism
vv	verses; violins
vv ll	(*variae lectiones*) variant readings
vy	various years (books)

W

W	West; Wales; Welsh
w	wife; week
WA	Western Australia
WAAC	Women's Army Auxiliary Corps
WAAF	Women's Auxiliary Air Force
Wadh	Wadham College (Oxford)
WAFF	West African Frontier Force
W & M	William and Mary (King William III and Queen Mary II)

WAR	West Africa Regiment
WC	West Central (postal district); water closet
WG	Welsh Guards
WHO	World Health Organisation
WI	West Indies; Women's Institute
W/Cdr	Wing Commander
WIR	West India Regiment
Wk	week
WLA	Women's Land Army
WLF	Women's Liberal Federation
WMO	World Meteorological Organisation
WMTC	Women's Mechanised Transport Corps
WNW	West-North-West
WO	War Office; Warrant Officer
Wp	Worship
WRAC	Women's Royal Army Corps
WRAF	Women's Royal Air Force
WRNS	Women's Royal Naval Service
WRVS	Women's Royal Voluntary Services
WS	Writer to the Signet (Scotland)
WSPU	Women's Social and Political Union
WSW	West-South-West
wt	weight
WVS	Women's Voluntary Services (now WRVS)

X

X	Christ; ten
x	unknown quantity (maths.)
xc (or xcp)	(Ex) without coupon
xd	(Ex) without dividend
xi	(Ex) without (next) interest payment
Xmas	Christmas
Xn	Christian
xn	(Ex) without the right to new shares
Xt	Christ
Xts	Christ's College (Cambridge)

Y

Y	year
y (or yd)	yard
YB	Year Book
Yd	Yard
Yeo	Yeomanry

YHA	Youth Hostels Association
YLI	Yorkshire Light Infantry
YMCA	Young Men's Christian Association
YM Cath A	Young Men's Catholic Association
YMCU	Young Men's Christian Union
YMFS	Young Men's Friendly Society
YPSCE	Young People's Society for Christian Endeavour
yr	year; your; younger
yrs	years; yours
yst	youngest
YWCA	Young Women's Christian Association
YWCTU	Young Women's Christian Temperance Union

Z

ZA	Zuid Afrika (South Africa)
ZETA	Zero Energy Thermonuclear Assembly
ZG	Zoological Gardens
Zool	Zoology
ZS	Zoological Society

A few of the foregoing abbreviations are now obsolete, but they are included in this list because they may all be encountered in literature.

For further lists of qualifications, see *British Qualifications*, a comprehensive guide to educational, technical, professional and academic qualifications in Britain. Compiled by Barbara Priestley and published by André Deutsch.

INDEX

(See also list of Contents at front of book)

Other Pan books that may interest you
are listed on the following pages

A Guide to Public Speaking 60p
R. Seton Lawrence

Here is a wealth of sound and practical advice, presented in a very readable form, with examples both of great oratory and of many pitfalls which can, with care, be avoided.

Recommended by many managerial and professional organizations.

The Story of Language 45p
C. L. Barber

'One of the best books of its kind to appear for years'
TIMES EDUCATIONAL SUPPLEMENT

Beginning with primitive man's first crude attempts at communication by sound, Dr Barber traces the development over thousands of years of organized language and its various families.

From the language groups emerging through the centuries he concentrates on the Indo-European as being of particular interest and describes the growth of the English language as we know it today. From each epoch – Old English, Middle English, the times of Chaucer, of Shakespeare, and later – he introduces pleasing examples of prose and verse to illustrate his arguments.

This edition of an important book is made still more valuable by revisions and additions, including the use of phonetic symbols from the international phonetic alphabet.

A Pan Original

Everyman's Roget's Thesaurus £1·25
Edited by D. C. Browning

Roget's Thesaurus is one of the English-speaking world's most valuable and celebrated works of reference. It is a treasury of synonyms, antonyms, parallel and related words, designed to help you find the right words or phrase to express your ideas with force and clarity.

This edition preserves the original plan of classification and categories (including the vast and ingenious index) and has been completely revised to bring all words and phrases into accordance with current usage. Over ten thousand more of these have been added, including many technical terms, everyday neologisms, Americanisms and slang.

'Among reference books *Roget's Thesaurus* stands by itself . . . a treasury upon which writers can draw'
THE TIMES LITERARY SUPPLEMENT

Chambers Essential English Dictionary 60p
Edited by A. M. MacDonald

A dictionary of the words essential to daily life, with clear, precise and informative definitions ; giving interesting derivations, illustrative examples of usage, and idiomatic expressions.

This is outstanding among small dictionaries for legibility and ease of reference. And although the background of our language makes up the body of the book, it fully reflects modern developments in words, meanings and outlook.

Waddingtons Family Card Games 45p
Robert Harbin

A pack of cards can give more fun than anything else; it is an endless source of enjoyment. In his book Robert Harbin demonstrates this as he entertainingly and clearly describes more than sixty card games, from traditional ones like Whist, Solo and Bridge, to the lesser known and even rare games such as Pishti, Cloboish and Solomon.

The Backgammon Book £1·00
Oswald Jacoby and John R. Crawford

A complete, up-to-date, step-by-step guide on how to play backgammon for love or money – and win.

Written by two world champions and illustrated with large, precise diagrams, this essential guide ranges from the crucial opening moves to the finer points of the middle and end games.

In addition to probability tables, etiquette and the official rules of the International Backgammon Association, there are chapters on the history of the game, how to run a tournament and how to play chouette (backgammon for more than two people), plus a useful glossary.